D1433147

WP Wakefield Libraries WP
& Information Services

- 1 OCT 2011

13 FEB 2012

- 2 JAN 2014

1 0 FEB 2014

3 0 NOV 2015

4 DEC 2015
1 8 FEB 2016
1 9 JAN 2018
1 NOV 2018

THE LIBRARY
HMP WAKEFIELD
5 LOVE LANE
WAKEFIELD
WF2 9AG

This book should be returned by the last date stamped above. You may renew the loan personally, by post or telephone for a further period if the book is not required by another reader.

WAKEFIELD LIBRARIES

30000010147469

TRAINING AND RACING THE
Greyhound

TRAINING AND RACING THE
Greyhound

Darren Morris

THE CROWOOD PRESS

First published in 2009 by
The Crowood Press Ltd
Ramsbury, Marlborough
Wiltshire SN8 2HR

www.crowood.com

© Darren Morris 2009

All rights reserved. No part of this publication may be reproduced or
transmitted in any form or by any means, electronic or mechanical,
including photocopy, recording, or any information storage and retrieval
system, without permission in writing from the publishers.

British Library Cataloguing-in-Publication Data
A catalogue record for this book is available from the British Library.

ISBN 978 1 84797 104 3

Photographic acknowledgement
The action photos in this book were supplied by Steve Nash. Steve has
specialized in greyhound racing photography since buying his own
greyhounds to race at the old Wembley Stadium back in 1984 and has been
Racing Post's greyhound photographer since the paper's launch in 1986.
His work has appeared internationally in numerous publications, books,
advertising campaigns, websites and other media, and can be viewed at
www.steve-nash.co.uk.

Disclaimer
The author and the publisher do not accept any responsibility in any
manner whatsoever for any error or omission, nor any loss, damage, injury,
or liability of any kind incurred as a result of the use of any of the
information contained in this book, or reliance upon it. This book is not in
any way intended to replace, or sidestep, the veterinary surgeon and, if in
doubt about any aspect of their dog's health, readers should seek
professional advice from a qualified veterinarian.

Cover: Ninja Jamie winning Derby Plate heats, Wimbledon Stadium,
24 May 2008. (© Steve Nash Photography)

Typeface used: New Century Schoolbook.

Typeset and designed by D & N Publishing
Baydon, Wiltshire.

Printed and bound in Malaysia by Times Offset (M) Sdn Bhd.

Contents

WAKEFIELD LIBRARIES & INFO. SERVICES	
30000010147469	
Bertrams	04/03/2011
636.753	£16.99

Acknowledgements

I have worked in the greyhound industry for over twenty years and during this time have benefited from the knowledge and expertise passed on to me by many of those with whom I have worked. Without their input I would never have gained the information that has enabled me to write this book.

The first trainer I worked for was the late Gerald Lilley; he was the only one who would give me a job when I was a small boy of thirteen. I then worked for Kevin Rushworth, Terry Townsend and George Curtis, who further extended my knowledge. Throughout my involvement with greyhounds I have always had a very keen interest in injuries, and I learned a great deal from the following vets and specialists: Plunkett Devlin, Ron Bradburn, Chris Backhouse, George Drake, Francis Allen, John Jenkins and Carol Patterson.

I would especially like to thank Laura Thorpe for her help with the photography, and Jackie and John Teal for their help over the last decade.

I would also like to thank my partner, Sophie, who strongly encouraged me to write this book, and who has shown incredible patience during the countless hours I have spent writing it.

Preface

The greyhound is a unique breed of dog; it has been around for thousands of years and has accompanied man as both hunter and companion. It is one of the fastest land mammals ever to grace our planet, and its speed has been used to hunt quarry around the globe. It has a laid back nature and loves attention, and this love is often returned unconditionally. Over the last century it has become better known as a racing dog, and it competes in races in many countries.

This book is aimed at the greyhound enthusiast, and contains information and advice on many different subjects, such as buying a dog to preparing a greyhound for a race; it covers several aspects of both racing and training. Issues such as feeding, anatomy and general care are all discussed to try and give the handler a closer look at this fascinating breed. At its heart is an in-depth chapter on injury diagnosis, and the accompanying problems that injuries may cause. Due to the physical stresses of racing and coursing, every greyhound will at some point sustain a fairly serious injury – indeed, minor injuries of some degree can be sustained every time the dog sets a paw on the track.

The book also takes a look at some of the serious and some of the not so serious complaints that a handler may need to diagnose. Unfortunately, it is often only in the later stages of injury or illness that a greyhound is actually taken to a veterinarian for treatment, when in some cases early diagnosis can be critical to the health of the dog. For this reason it is important that the trainer works in close conjunction with his veterinarian.

Whether you're a novice handler or a professional trainer of long standing, I am sure that *Training and Racing the Greyhound* has something to offer.

*Lenson Joker racing at Wimbledon in 2008. This dog was voted
2008 Greyhound of the Year, the sport's highest honour.*
(© Steve Nash Photography)

CHAPTER ONE

The Greyhound and Greyhound Racing

ABOUT THE GREYHOUND

The greyhound is a medium to large breed of dog and can vary a great deal in both size and shape. At its smallest a bitch may weigh as little as 20kg (44lb), but a male dog may well tip the scales at anything up to 40kg (88lb). It can also be contrasting in shape, as some are tall and lean while others are short and stocky. But while size and shape can differ, its general characteristics are always easily distinguishable from any other breed, typically the long snout, deep chest, well tucked up abdomen, and the heavy musculature covering its frame. In its prime the greyhound should be well muscled and should look like an athlete in every sense of the word. Its strong, solid and pronounced musculature should be covered by very little fat, giving that rippling effect as it moves.

The greyhound's coat is short, and because of this it is easily manageable: grooming, bathing and massaging can be readily accomplished even by the novice. Most pedigree breeds come in one or two colours; however, the greyhound is different and comes in a wide variety of markings and colours. First there is the plain dog that is a straight colour such as black, blue, brindle, fawn and occasionally all white or

A white and brindle dog; notice that the white is greater than the brindle.

chocolate – though for the greyhound even these straight colours can have a variation, such as red fawn, blue fawn, blue brindle, silver brindle, light brindle and dark brindle. Second there is the coloured dog, which is basically white but with patches covering parts of it; the easiest way to describe it is to compare it to the markings of a dairy cow. The patches are most commonly black or fawn in colour, but blue and brindle patches are still plentiful.

As a rule the greyhound is placid and laid back in nature, and almost never shows any sign of aggression, especially towards a human; it is often happy to sleep for most of the day, as it loves nothing more than to chill out and relax. However, it must be understood that the greyhound is also a hunter by nature, and if provoked can get excited very quickly, especially in a kennel or pack environment. It is both strong and highly mobile, so it is important that the handler keeps his wits about him at all times; if you are caught off your guard, a greyhound can easily pull you off your feet.

As the greyhound has been bred to hunt, the handler must understand that small animals moving quickly in the line of sight are very likely to be chased. If your greyhound is being exercised with other dogs, then it is important to take precautions; for instance, always keep a dog muzzled, and never exercise more dogs than you can control.

Although the greyhound is not considered to be very intelligent when compared to other breeds of dog, it makes up for it in other ways. It has an abundance of speed and sheer enthusiasm when asked to perform a task. Its body is toned and conditioned like no other breed, allowing it to reach speeds in excess of 64km/h (40mph); this makes it one of the fastest land mammals on earth. It also loves attention, and will equally happily give its affection to everyone and anyone it comes into contact with. It rarely shows total loyalty to one person or master.

Altogether the greyhound is a remarkable animal, which is why many different breeds of dog are crossed with it, the idea being to breed in a little more intelligence to accompany the speed. These cross-bred dogs are known as lurchers, and are themselves remarkable animals.

A LITTLE GREYHOUND HISTORY

The greyhound is the most ancient breed of dog. Paintings and murals have been found dating back well over 4,000 years; it has even been noted that a mummified dog with the attributes of a greyhound was found in a tomb dating back to 6000BC. The greyhound is the only dog to be mentioned in the Bible.

Over the centuries there have been many cultures that have truly admired our beloved greyhound, such as the Egyptians, the Persians and the Greeks. The Egyptians held it in the utmost respect and gave it almost god-like status; it was kept both as a pet and a hunter, but many of the kings and high hierarchy would pitch their greyhounds against each other in races chasing wild game – to have a fast hound may well have brought favour in the king's eyes. Many Egyptians have greyhounds portrayed in their tombs, and when you consider that only things of significance were selected for portrayal here, then it must be assumed that the greyhound was regarded as highly important.

Throughout ancient history the Greeks and the Romans are both associated with the greyhound; even many of the Greek gods are portrayed with one. The Romans loved their greyhounds too, and are known to have enjoyed coursing; however, they often ran their dogs for the thrill of the chase alone, and not for hunting for food.

Like the Egyptians, the Arabians held the greyhound in very high esteem, and it became much sought after; it was the only dog permitted to ride with them on their camels, and also to be allowed into their tents.

In the Middle Ages the greyhound became almost extinct during times of famine; it was rescued from this almost certain fate by clergymen. It was then cared for and bred by the nobility; in the tenth century King Howel

A greyhound at play.

and in June 1927 the great White City in London opened its doors for the first time; soon it was said to be attracting an estimated 100,000 people per meeting. Greyhound racing was born.

GREYHOUND RACING

Greyhound racing was brought to England by the American Charles Munn, who had the overseas rights to the mechanical lure or hare. The first track was opened at Belle Vue, and it made so much money that further tracks at Harringay and White City were soon being planned.

With the sport becoming increasingly popular and the potential for malpractice becoming ever greater, the promoters of many of the tracks held a meeting at Wembley to discuss the founding of a nationally controlled organization. It was agreed unanimously that a greyhound club along the lines of the horse racing jockey club should be set up. The motion was passed, and the club was formed on 23 April 1928. At this point in time forty-three tracks agreed to be regulated under the legislation of the newly founded club, known as the National Greyhound Racing Club, or the NGRC.

Greyhound racing continued to flourish, and became extremely popular with the working class, who found the urban locations and the evening race cards convenient for their life-style. Owners and patrons from all walks of life came racing, and the sport became very popular among gamblers; even today gambling is arguably the backbone of the greyhound racing industry.

Greyhound racing reached its peak in attendances shortly after World War II, but since then it has suffered a downward spiral largely because of the legalisation of off-course betting (betting shops), televised sports coverage, and most recently the introduction of Internet betting. All these facilities make it far easier for the punter to place bets to his heart's content without ever leaving the comfort of his own home. However, greyhound racing has always had strong grass roots and is still popular throughout the world in all walks of life.

declared that killing a greyhound would be punishable by death. During these times most dogs were considered of no value and almost treated as vermin; however, by contrast the greyhound was seen as elegant and noble.

In the 1500s Queen Elizabeth I initiated the first formal rules of hare coursing, and these rules were still in use when the first official coursing club was set up in 1776 at Swaffham.

In the nineteenth century the greyhound was still favoured among the nobility and royalty, with greyhound coursing becoming even more popular; the Waterloo Cup was founded in 1837. It was during this period that the greyhound was imported to the United States to help in the control of the jack rabbit, which was wreaking havoc in the crop fields.

In July 1926 the first ever greyhound race meeting was held at Belle Vue in Manchester,

Ballymac Touser, Trap 4 (right of shot), leading Da Vinci Smiler (Trap 5, left), Peterborough Stadium, 19 July 2008. (© Steve Nash Photography)

Ballybeg Honcho leading at the first bend in the Champions Night Puppy heats, Romford Stadium, in July 2002. (© Steve Nash Photography)

It is the second largest spectator sport in England, with tracks spread over the length and breadth of the country. Because of its popularity, racing takes place on seven days a week, with meetings being run morning, noon and night to cope with the heavy demand of both punters and bookmakers.

Greyhound racing also takes place around the world with Ireland, Australia and America being leading countries in the greyhound industry.

In England, Scotland and Wales there are tracks governed by the NGRC (National Greyhound Racing Club), but as well as these there are also independent tracks run under their own rules and regulations. It is somewhat similar to horse racing, where there are professional trainers who run under Jockey Club rules at recognized race tracks, and then point to point meetings run under the auspices of the local Hunt and held at local courses.

Racing under the NGRC is run under strict rules, and the dogs' welfare is closely scrutinized. The trainers will have their kennels checked on a yearly basis by a designated racing steward to make sure they are up to standard. Each and every trainer, kennel hand, track official and member of track staff will have to have a licence to operate or work at an NGRC track. A veterinary surgeon will be present at every race meeting to check each dog for injury or illness, and the dogs are regularly drug tested to prevent trainers from using illegal substances.

On the independent circuit each track is run by its own set of rules, which vary from one track to another. A trainer needs no official licence, and indeed anyone who owns a greyhound can turn up and race his dog. These tracks rarely have veterinary supervision on site, and drug testing is never undertaken. Over the years these tracks have been exceptionally popular, and until recently there have been dozens of them spread over the length and breadth of the country. However, over the last twenty years the price of building land has been high, and sadly many of them have been sold off for building development.

There are two types of race for a greyhound to compete in, depending on its ability: graded events, which are races where six dogs of equal ability are pitched against each other; and open events, where any dog may enter – though these races are generally aimed at the better class of dog. Each track also has a racing manager or management team, responsible for its day-to-day running.

The Racing Manager

The racing manager is also in charge of the day-to-day racing programme; it is therefore his job to assess the greyhounds competing at his track, and to grade or rank them accordingly. When any dog has a trial or race at a track it is timed by an electronic timing system, and this enables the racing manager to assess accurately how fast each greyhound is. He must also place each greyhound in the trap he thinks will suit it best, according to its trials or races.

When the manager is happy with a greyhound's trial or trials, it will then be made available for the racing strength, and it is from this criterion that he selects the dogs to make up each race. It is ultimately his aim to place six dogs of equal ability into a race, and get them to finish as close together as possible at the winning line.

Trials

When a new greyhound is taken to a track it must compete in three trial runs so that the racing manager can assess its ability. A trial is basically a timed run around the track, and the dog can then be graded or placed into a race with dogs of a similar speed, judged according to the times they achieved in their trials. When a greyhound has been off the track with an injury, the racing manager will often require that it also has a trial run before it can be made available to run in a race again.

While in the majority of trial runs three greyhounds will take part, in the case of a dog having its first run at a new track, most trainers prefer to give a solo trial (with just the one dog). This is because many of the tracks, especially those in England, are totally different in size and shape, and if a dog has a solo run it can have a good look at the track before it competes with other dogs. A solo trial is also often preferable when a greyhound is having its first trial back after being injured, because it then has the chance to have a clean run without being bumped about by others.

Graded Races

Once a greyhound has had its three grading trials, and provided it is fast enough to compete, then it will be allowed on to the racing strength or quota. It is from this racing strength that the racing manager compiles his races, which usually range over about ten different levels. The track and its racing strength will largely influence how many levels or grades of racing it has. These levels are usually numbered from one upwards, and the lower the number, the better the class of dog; grade one therefore always includes the best dogs on the track.

In graded racing there are three different distances at each track: sprint races, standard races, and long distance races. Standard races are generally around 500m, and make up a large portion of the greyhound races that take place in England. Sprint races and long-distance races are often added to the racing card to supply a bit of variety.

Handicap Racing

Handicap racing is when dogs of different levels of ability are all placed into the same graded race. Each greyhound has its own starting trap and receives a designated number of metres' start from the 'scratch' dog. Thus the best dog in the race runs from scratch, or the furthest trap back, then each trap is set at a distance in metres, as decided by the racing manager. For example:

Trap 1: Billy the Kid	Receives 13m
Trap 2: Sam the Baker	Receives 10m
Trap 3: Mr Fish	Receives 8m
Trap 4: Honey Bunny	Receives 6m
Trap 5: Treacle Tart	Receives 4m
Trap 6: Roach's Pride	Scratch

On the independent circuit most of the racing is run in this way, the handicap form. Some greyhounds, especially puppies, gain a serious advantage at being put at the front of a handicap, because they then have a good chance of seeing the hare or lure without getting bumped and tipped about. It must also be appreciated that some greyhounds don't chase the hare properly, and these dogs often benefit from chasing poorer quality dogs. In normal flat races they may well hit the lead too early and will then wait for another dog to run alongside, whereas in the handicap race they often have dogs way out in front to chase, which means they don't catch them until near the finish, so they actually run a much better race.

Open Races

In open races the best dogs race at various tracks up and down the country. Unlike in graded events where a greyhound will race at the same track on a weekly basis, the open race dog will travel from track to track, depending on where the open races are taking place. Generally a track will advertise an open race or competition, the trainer will enter his greyhound, and the racing manager will then pick the best six greyhounds out of those that have been entered to make up the race.

As well as single open races there are often open competitions where heats, quarter finals, semi-finals and a final may well be run. These events are often of great financial and prestigious benefit to the winning trainer and dog.

Open races are like graded racing in that the races involve a broad spectrum of distances. As well as sprinting, standard and long-distance races, there are also marathon races, which are anything up to 1,000m.

Types of Hare

In greyhound racing the dogs chase a mechanical hare that runs around the inside or the outside of the track. In the early days of racing the majority of tracks ran with a hare on the inner circumference of the track; however, as time has moved on, many of the tracks have changed to a hare system where the hare runs around the outer edge of the race circuit.

There are two types of hare system in use today: first, the Sumner hare system, which runs above the ground on a rail; the hare itself is situated on a short metal arm, usually on the inside of the track. Secondly there is the McGhee hare that runs on a rail situated in the ground; this system is always on the outside of the track. The McGhee hare runs along the ground in a more life-like manner.

Interestingly, some greyhounds will only chase one type of hare system. If a puppy is schooled or has learnt to run on one type of hare system it will sometimes not chase the other type. Some dogs will chase one type of hare 100 per cent, but when put behind the other hare they may well not chase it properly. This is often seen in greyhounds that play and fight with the leading dog of the race; they tend to run with the other dogs, and don't chase the hare.

Greyhound Coursing

Greyhound coursing has taken place for thousands of years, but the Hunting Act, passed by Parliament in 2004, made it illegal to hunt with dogs; this included fox hunting, the hunting of deer, hares and mink, and organized hare coursing. The Act came into operation in England and Wales in February 2005. Greyhound coursing involved two greyhounds being pitched against live quarry in an open field designated specifically for this purpose. Hare coursing was not about killing hares, but about determining which dogs exhibited the most agility and the highest speed. Thus two dogs would compete against each other in a chase after live quarry, and the dog with the most points proceeded to the next round until a winner was declared.

Coventry Bees winning at Hove Stadium, 21 March 2008 (Good Friday meeting).
(© Steve Nash Photography)

CHAPTER TWO

Basic Care
and Training

If you have just purchased your first greyhound, or if you have just started working with greyhounds for the first time, then the prospect of handling them can be quite daunting. Most are laid back in nature, but when put in a kennel environment the greyhound can become a pack animal, and in training it can quickly become excitable, its laid-back nature changing in an instant. Indeed in training it can be a very Jekyll and Hyde character: while generally of a genuine, loving nature, it must be understood that it is also a natural hunter.

A young pup looks upon his squabbling siblings.

BASIC HANDLING TECHNIQUES

Because of the greyhound's nature, it is important that the novice handler gets the basic handling techniques right – even collaring up a dog or feeding it can risk injury to both dog and handler if it is not done correctly. Loose dogs can cause fights, they can run into objects or people, or a nervous dog may break free and you may not be able to catch it. Here I will discuss some of the basic but important facts and techniques that a handler should observe.

Basic Control

Putting a collar and lead on a dog may seem an easy task, but it still needs to be done correctly. The best type of collar is a wide 'fish' collar, as a dog finds it much harder to pull its head through these; when a greyhound gets excited it has a tendency to turn and pull its head through the collar and slip the lead. The collar should be put on round the top of the neck just behind the ears and fastened tightly, but with enough slack to get your index and middle finger underneath it. It helps if the lead has a swivel on it to prevent it getting twisted and tangled.

The following facts and techniques regarding control should also be observed:

- It is important that you have full control over the dog at all times; if it gets free then it may well injure itself or other dogs in the immediate vicinity.

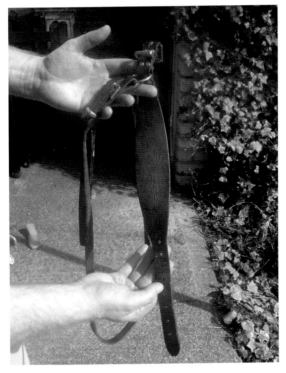

A fish collar; notice its thickness, which helps to reduce the chances of the dog slipping it.

A swivel lead; this helps greatly with dogs that turn around frequently while on the lead.

- If a dog turns itself and tries to slip the lead, it is important not to let the lead get tight: do your best to follow the dog, all the while coaxing it to calm it down. It is when the lead is pulled tight that the dog can get some leverage and slip its head through the collar.
- When walking a greyhound in public, and in particular when walking more than one, it should be muzzled. A large box muzzle should be used, and put on so that the muzzle is tight, but not so tight that the nose is pressed against the front. While I would consider this essential for any dog in training, a greyhound that is retired from racing should soon calm down, and the use of a muzzle may well not be needed. However, always proceed cautiously.
- When bending over a dog to examine it or to clip its nails, it is advisable to keep it muzzled. It is also advisable to position your arm between your face and the dog's mouth, because if you happen to cause the dog a little pain, even the most placid might turn round for a nip.
- When getting a greyhound out of a kennel it should always be done with your foot or knee held firmly behind the door to stop the dog pushing past you and escaping. Greyhounds are generally kennelled in pairs, and while one dog is being collared up, the other may well be trying to escape. A loose dog is always an accident waiting to happen.
- If a greyhound is running at you, or is loose and is running in your direction, then spread your arms and move backwards; and if it doesn't begin to slow you may have to retreat a little faster. As the dog comes past you, try to grab it, but go with it as you do so: it is not wise to rugby tackle it because you could do the dog or yourself – or both – serious damage. Similarly, if you stand still and a dog runs into you, then you may be seriously

A box muzzle; this is used not because the greyhound is vicious in nature, but because it tends to get excited very quickly when in training.

injured: more than once I have seen a handler suffer a broken leg when struck by a fast-moving greyhound.

- When a greyhound is loose, never chase it, because it will always run away from you, but always try and coax it back, especially if it is nervy; walking or jogging away from it will often encourage it to follow. If it is extremely nervous you may have to get another dog to try and coax it back to you; and if a familiar dog or kennel companion doesn't work, you may have to resort to coaxing it with food.
- The use of excessive force on a dog is not necessary; a naughty greyhound will not come into line by slapping it. The only time a dog should be hit is in the unlikely event of a fight, when you may need to use whatever comes to hand to break them up. If possible a bucket of cold water should be slung over the brawling dogs, though the down side of this is that it takes time to fill a bucket of water, and it might be critical to get the dogs separated without any such delay.

Feeding Guidelines

- When two dogs are kennelled together, you should feed them separately. If they are fed together they may well fight, nor do you

know exactly how much food each dog is consuming. Place one food bowl outside the kennel and open the door to let one of the dogs out, then place the other bowl inside. Once a dog gets used to feeding outside, then it will usually come out for its food with few problems. If you have a new dog it may be advisable to put a lead on it in order to bring it out of the kennel.
- When collaring up a dog to feed it outside its kennel it is advisable to place the end of the lead over its back. Some dogs are very overprotective of their food, and if you bend over the dog first to collar it up, you risk being bitten in the face. By placing the lead on its back, if it does have a little snap then you are standing up and ready to deal with the situation.
- If you are working in a larger kennel environment, never feed the dogs that are outside their kennels too close together, but always leave enough space between them so they can't get near to each other. Also, never walk a dog past another that is feeding; greyhounds can be very aggressive in proximity to their food, especially in a kennel environment.
- When the dog has finished feeding, always move the bowl away from it with your foot before you bend down to pick it up.

- While the greyhound is a soft, lovable, human-friendly dog, it is always best to err on the side of caution when working around any breed of dog and food. Thus, if you bend down to pick up the dog's bowl without first moving it away with your foot, you unintentionally risk your face being bitten.

Basic Exercising and Travel Guidelines

- When walking greyhounds you should never walk any more dogs than you can handle. I have seen trainers let very slightly built handlers walk sets of eight dogs. If a rabbit pops up or a loose dog runs into the set, then what chance does the handler have of staying in control? I would suggest that four dogs are enough for any one person to handle safely.
- In the summer months when the days are hot, exercise your dogs in the morning and in the evening to avoid any heat-related problems. Over-exposure to the sun can be a killer, so there is no point risking their health by exercising them in the heat of the day. Black dogs always seem to suffer the worst as the colour black absorbs heat.
- When travelling on a hot day, always ensure that your transport is well ventilated, and be sure to park it out of the direct sunlight. Never leave a dog in a car on a sunny day: a dog can die of heat stroke in a very short period of time.
- When a greyhound has raced, it is important to let it catch its tongue before it is put on a transport or in a car; in warm weather it could be dead by the time you get back to your kennels.

Rules around the Kennels

- Any dog that is ill through sickness or disease should be quarantined as best as possible. Many illnesses are highly contagious, and you should do your very best to stop any contact between your greyhounds. Many larger kennels often have their own quarantine block.
- Never let young children run around in the kennel or the kennel environment; the greyhound can become excited very quickly, and accidents need to be avoided when possible.
- Wheelbarrows and other such objects should be moved out of walkways and kennel areas after use. The greyhound can often be clumsy, and could do itself a lot of damage if it inadvertently walks into such objects.

A greyhound in transit. It is an advantage if the vehicle is caged out so greyhounds are kept separate while travelling; this also prevents them moving and falling about while the vehicle is in motion.

- Always keep your kennels clean and tidy, disinfect them at least once a day, and always try and clean up any kennel mess swiftly. Leaving faeces in a kennel not only causes bad odours, but can spread germs and disease.

THE BASIC TRAINING OF GREYHOUNDS

There are differing definitions of a good greyhound trainer. Firstly, some people may be under the impression that because you have a very large bank balance and can afford to buy top class animals, then you must be a good trainer. However, a testament to this misconception is the number of good dogs that are put into early retirement because of the trainer's ignorance. If you can afford to buy very expensive dogs it won't matter how bad a trainer you are, because you will still win races, for a while.

Secondly, some people believe that trainers who can pull a large betting gamble must be very good. However, there have been some trainers, and no doubt there will be others, who have used certain pharmaceutical compounds to slow down, or speed up, their dogs. This despicable practice is, of course, illegal, and those who engage in these practices are the antithesis of what constitutes a good trainer.

In my opinion being a good greyhound trainer is about knowing your dogs and being able to give them a decent level of care. It is also important that you have a good knowledge of illness and injury so that your dogs are given proper attention and treatment. Being able to condition a dog and bring him to peak fitness at the right time is another aspect of becoming a good trainer; thus preparing a dog for a particular competition or certain race is a skill that needs to be mastered. When you can land a gamble through your own initiative and hard work, then maybe you can start to think that you can train a little bit.

If you are to become an accomplished trainer it is important that certain key areas in your training regime are set up correctly, and that all the criteria for good management are fulfilled.

Two greyhounds turned out within a large paddock.

The Kennels

A good starting point is to ensure a clean environment in which to keep your dogs. The bed should be spacious and have a plentiful supply of fresh bedding. As previously explained, any dog mess should be cleaned up promptly to combat the spread of germs and to try and keep the kennels smelling relatively pleasant. In summer the kennels should be well ventilated to prevent the occupants overheating. In winter the dogs should be kept warm with a generous supply of bedding, and you should put coats on the dogs, whether they are feeling the cold or not.

Feeding

Learning how to feed your dogs correctly is a major part of your training. Not only will you have to adjust what you feed according to whether the dog needs to pick up in condition or be let down, but you must also experiment to try and find each dog's best racing weight. Some dogs will run well with a good healthy back, whereas others are better when they are much leaner. It is also important that your dogs are given a good supply of vitamins, minerals and other supplements, especially when they are sick or lame.

Exercise

How you exercise your dogs will also have a major effect on how they perform. Walking and galloping routines can be used to bring your dogs into condition, but great care must be taken as too much or too little work can be counter-productive. It is also important that your dogs are let out frequently so they can relieve themselves; some will contain themselves all night if they must, which is not a healthy situation for them.

Managing Injury

Having a good knowledge of the greyhound's anatomy, and learning how to examine and treat your dog correctly, can have a considerable bearing on your success as a trainer. Failing to identify injuries, and running dogs that are lame in one form or another, can lead to frustration for the handler. Injuries are often more complicated than most trainers and even vets, would realize, and by taking the time to extend your knowledge of injuries and how to treat them will reap its own rewards.

As with any dog, it is important that you learn about, and can recognize, some of the minor and major ailments. If a dog develops or contracts a serious illness such as gastroenteritis or septicaemia it is important that it is examined by a veterinarian at an early stage; some conditions can be fatal, so it should be seen before it is in the later stages of an illness.

Minor problems will often not need veterinary attention but as a trainer you should know some basic first aid and have some decent kit in case of any accidents. Small bites, cuts and grazes are inevitable in kennels and it is therefore important to be prepared.

Training the Individual

Most important is that you treat each dog as an individual and that you don't train every dog the same way. Some dogs benefit from lots of exercise, others don't. Some benefit from certain supplements; some need worming more regularly than others; some run well on a high protein diet, others are pushed over the top and underperform. Some dogs run well heavy or carrying extra weight, while others need to have their weight kept light; some run well after a short break or lay-off from racing. It is often just by experimenting a little that you will find what best suits each dog.

I feel that if you can keep your dogs happy, comfortable and give them the attention that they deserve, then you should take pride in yourself for that.

KENNELLING

The NGRC (National Greyhound Racing Club) is the governing body of greyhound racing in England, Scotland and Wales. Under the NGRC there are certain regulations on how your kennels should be set up to get them licensed. If you run your greyhounds on the independent circuit then you can basically kennel your dog as you please. However, if you keep to the rules as a good solid guideline then your kennels should be perfectly acceptable.

These are the guidelines of the NGRC requirements for your kennels:

- A kennel should not house more than two greyhounds. (The majority of trainers like to kennel their dogs in mixed sex pairs.)
- Buildings should be preferably made out of brick, concrete or breeze-blocks.
- The kennel should have 2m headroom and should be a minimum of 2.3m in depth and 1.5m wide.
- The bed should be a minimum of 1sq m, and 20cm off the floor.
- There should be a minimum of 1.25m between the bed and the front of the kennel.
- Reasonable precautions should be taken for quarantine so that you can separate any dogs that are poorly.
- Your kennels should have access to clean fresh water. They should also have an electricity supply and a 'phone.

Time to relax after a hard day.

A basic kennel; paper bedding is preferred to straw; it is cleaner, odourless and far less dusty. Saw dust is preferred for the floor; in winter it helps prevent a dog acquiring a chill when lying on the floor.

- Any necessary measures should be taken to control vermin.
- Except for greyhounds, no other live animals are allowed on the kennel premises.

When setting up your kennels there are some other useful things that you can do:

- When designing the bed don't make the front too high; a metal rim can also be placed over the top edge of the bed to stop the dogs chewing the wood.
- A partition can be made to slide down the centre of the bed, and designed so that it can be removed easily. While some dogs get on well together, there is always the occasional bully, and the partition can be used to separate any aggressive dogs.
- The bed should be made so it can be taken apart easily for cleaning, both the bed itself and underneath it. Some dogs regularly wet the bed so a quick and effective method of dismantling and cleaning it can be useful.
- When making the door be sure to leave a 5cm (2in) gap at its base, to prevent dogs' paws getting injured. Also leave a small gap where

the door closes: if it closes flush then a tail can easily be caught in it, and damaged.

- If your kennel floors are concrete then it is advisable to coat the floor lightly with sawdust or shavings, as some dogs like to lie on the floor and can easily get a chill if they sleep on cold concrete.
- Your kennels should be well ventilated so that dogs don't get overhot in warm conditions. In the summer months the windows can be covered with light material to block out some sunlight to keep the kennels cooler.
- Heating and adequate bedding should be supplied in the winter months to keep your dogs warm. Some trainers prefer not to use heating, but it is important to take the chill off your kennels, even if you don't necessarily heat them up.
- Your kennels should have an adequately spacious kitchen where food can be prepared. The most important prerequisite is cleanliness. Worktops, bowls, mincer, fridges and so on, should be meticulously washed and cleaned to help prevent illness and disease.

Any food should be kept in containers or the fridge to protect against flies and vermin.

- Flies can be a real nuisance: not only do they irritate your dogs but they spread germs and disease. Measures should be taken to try and help prevent flies getting into your kennel, and also to try and destroy any flies that have got in.
- Vermin such as mice and rats can also be a problem, and it is usually much easier to use traps at the first sign of infestation. If you do need to use poison then it is imperative that it is placed where your dogs can't possibly get at it. You must also be aware that it is much easier for a dog to kill a dopey, half-poisoned rat, so you must be vigilant.

Turnout Runs

Most kennels have small concrete turnout paddocks or runs where you can put your dogs out to do their toilet duties. These runs are better suited if they have a slight camber and run off into a drainage system; this makes it a lot easier to wash down the run without leaving

A small run is ideal for dogs to relieve themselves without being able to run around. Notice the run is on a slight gradient so it can be washed down easily without leaving any standing water.

A fawn bitch blows off steam.

A black coursing greyhound relaxing in the paddock.

any surface water. The surrounding walls or fencing should be designed so the dog can't jump up or over and injure himself.

The runs should be cleaned of any faeces and disinfected between dogs entering the run, to help reduce any cross contamination. Some dogs also have a dirty habit of eating other dog's faeces if you give them the opportunity. As well as the small turn-out runs, most kennels should have larger grass paddocks where dogs can be let out. These paddocks should be fenced with suitable fencing and a concrete area should be made available, preferably near the gate in case of muddy conditions. It is important to check the paddocks on a daily basis for any objects that may cause injury, also any holes should be filled in to prevent serious leg injuries.

CHAPTER THREE

Breeding and Early Training

Breeding and rearing are in themselves a complicated business, and a specialist breeder could write a whole book on the subject. For the purpose of this book I shall give just a brief overview.

BREEDING

Breeding a litter of pups is a decision that should not be taken lightly. The cost alone can run into thousands of pounds with injections, registrations, feeding and worming, not to mention any vet bills that you might incur. But if

Two young puppies. It's hard work, you know.

you are determined to breed a litter, then it is important that you spend your money wisely and use a good quality stud dog that is a proven sire. An extra few hundred pounds is nothing when you compare it to the cost of rearing a litter of pups up to racing age. If you are a novice breeder then you may well want to take professional advice on the best stud dog that will suit your bitch.

Breed from the Best

If you are serious about breeding a litter then it is important that you only breed from a top-class bitch, or a bitch with very good blood lines. It is widely thought that the bitch influences 70 to 80 per cent of the pup's makeup, and the stud dog only the smaller percentage. When you consider the large amount of money it is going to cost you to rear a litter, then it is important that the bitch you breed from is good quality.

As an example, when the legendary Ballyreagan Bob first went to stud he threw a lot of inferior quality dogs and was therefore gaining a poor reputation. However, the main problem was that he was covering a lot of poor quality bitches because everyone wanted a litter by the great dog; if you took a closer look, some of the good bitches he covered actually produced some decent pups, even though he had a lot of poor young dogs racing at the time.

When the bitch and the sire have been chosen you need to have a good idea when the bitch is due to break season (come on heat) so that you can book her in with the stud dog you want. You may need to have three or four

26

choices, as the best stud dogs can be booked up months in advance and may have a full book.

It is also wise to have the bitch checked over by a veterinarian to rule out any possible breeding problems with the bitch such as genetic problems, temperament problems, heart condition and allergies, and also for worming and vaccination advice.

The mating procedure will usually be supervised by the professional stud-dog keeper or the owner. The stud dog may cover many bitches each month, and mating generally proceeds without complication. If the bitch is being sent to Ireland to be mated to an Irish stud dog you may be required to leave the bitch with them for a couple of days.

With today's technology there have been major advances in the use of artificial insemination, when the sperm of the stud dog is collected under clinical conditions, then chilled or frozen and sent to the home premises of the bitch, and inserted into the bitch at the right time of oestrous.

Care of the Pregnant Bitch

After the bitch has been mated it is good practice to supplement her diet with calcium in order to maintain normal calcium levels in the mother and achieve optimum bone development in the puppies.

The pups should arrive on about the sixty-second or sixty-third day from the day of the mating; however, early or late pregnancies are not unusual.

Within a week or ten days of the bitch being due she should be put in her whelping kennel so she can settle in. The kennel should be clean, quiet and have good lighting and ventilation. By this stage the bitch's belly should be quite large, and her teats should be filling with milk. She should be eating plenty; it is better policy to give her frequent small meals (four or five a day) rather than one large one, due to the pressure of the puppies filling her abdomen.

A quality heat lamp should be purchased and made ready for the arrival of the pups; how much or how often you will need to use it will largely depend on the time of year and the ambient temperature. It must be noted that in the first week puppies cannot shiver to keep warm, so it is essential that a heat lamp is used.

For the last week before the birth any bedding should be disposed of and replaced with sheets of old newspaper. These can be removed and replaced quickly and easily, which is necessary because they will get messed up during the birth. Bedding should not be used as the pups could well get tangled up in it and suffocate; furthermore bedding is a much greater fire risk if there is any sort of problem with the heat lamp.

Prior to the birth it is a good idea to notify your vet of the date the bitch is due.

Giving Birth

It is important that during the birth the bitch is supervised at all times; it is not unusual for this to take place throughout the night, so the things you will need should be made ready beforehand, such as towels, newspapers, disinfectant, a heat lamp and coffee. For the handler who is whelping down his first litter I would suggest that he seeks assistance from someone who has prior experience of what to do.

When the bitch is due to start whelping she will start to 'nest', will pant rather heavily, and look restless. When she actually starts giving birth, nature usually takes its course and the bitch is usually calmer than the handler. If it is her first litter she may well be unsure of what to do, and may need a little help.

A pup may or may not be born within the birth sac. The bitch will normally break the bag if necessary and chew the umbilical cord. You may need to assist the bitch if she is showing no signs of aiding the newborn. If necessary clear the bag and break the cord about 12cm from the puppy. It is unwise to use a sharp implement, as a straight cut may cause the cord to bleed unduly. Your fingers may well be sufficient. Clear the mouth of any mucus and rub the puppy with a towel; then make the bitch aware of the puppy by placing it close to the mother's head.

It is also important that the handler keeps an eye on the length of time between each pup

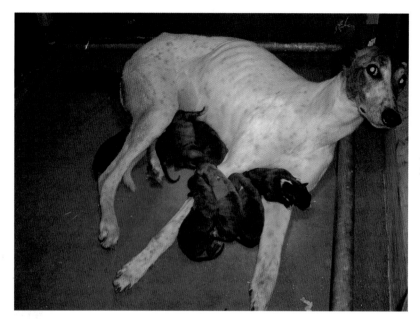

A proud mum with her young puppies.

being born. How long it takes for each pup to be born varies, but generally the interval between each one should not be more than two to three hours. If the bitch is having contractions but showing no signs of passing a pup, then you should seek the assistance of your vet.

After the birth the bitch should be cleaned down with warm water and allowed to pass urine/faeces. The bed should be cleaned off, and all the newspaper should be changed: it is important to try and keep the area as clean as possible to avoid any infection. Note that it is normal for the bitch to pass a dark green discharge for several days, and that bleeding may be evident for anything up to three weeks after the birth.

When the pups are born they should be able to suckle naturally, and it is important that they feed well not only because they need to fill their stomach, but because for the first day or two the mother passes vital protective antibodies to her pups in her milk (this 'first milk' is known as colostrum). Your assistance may again be needed at this point with a first-time mother because she may be fidgety, and you may need to help the weaker pups to find her teats and get sucking.

It takes about ten days for the pups to open their eyes; by this time they should be well away, and rolling and crawling about.

REARING THE PUPPIES

After the birth the bitch will usually lose a vast amount of weight, so she should be allowed to eat as much as she requires. It is essential to feed her several times a day because she requires a high level of calories to feed her puppies.

It is important that the handler keeps a close eye on the discharge passed by the mother; if this appears to be an excessive amount and it smells bad it could be a sign of infection, and veterinary advice should be sought as soon as possible.

In the early stages the handler should make sure the pups are warm, are getting enough milk, and are kept in a clean environment. It is also important that the mother is not taken away from the pups for too long, as this can be very stressful for both mother and pups. You should keep a watchful eye on her teats to make sure she is producing enough milk, and that the pups are not cutting her up and

Even at several weeks old the puppies still love mum's milk.

making her sore if their nails are sharp; these should be clipped back frequently to prevent this happening.

The puppies will require no extra feeding until they reach around six weeks of age. For the first couple of weeks of weaning the pups may well need feeding three or four times a day on top of the milk their mother provides. The first meals should be liquid – starting with milk and progressing to gravy, for example – and then solids can be gradually increased as the puppy's digestive system matures. When feeding the pups always make sure that the mother is kept well out of the way.

Worming

Roundworms are a common problem in the young puppy; an infected pup will often have a very large belly, and will probably be suffering from diarrhoea and be vomiting. A pup should be wormed at around two weeks old, and then at two- or three-week intervals until it is three or four months old. A puppy wormer should be obtained from your veterinarian and given as prescribed. It is important that you worm the puppies regularly even if you think that they don't have worms.

TEACHING THE GREYHOUND PUPPY TO RACE

Puppies do not learn to run around a greyhound track all by themselves. While it is natural for them to chase live quarry across a field, chasing a dummy hare often needs plenty of tuition. There are many different methods used by trainers to school their pups. Some start them off at a very early age, and by the time they are fifteen months old they are fit and raring to go; others like to leave them, and they are often still wandering around a field in Ireland at sixteen months old. Personally I think it is preferable to stick to the middle way.

In the greyhound world puppies are still classed as puppies until they are two years of age; their bones and structure are not fully developed until this time, so too frequent running at an early age can undoubtedly lead to problems. On the other hand, pups that are left doing nothing until they are eighteen months sometimes do struggle to get to grips with the whole concept of racing.

By the time the pups are six months of age they should be separated from their siblings,

Hello! Where's mum?

Wakey wakey, is that my dinner coming? The pups race from their shelter for their breakfast.

and exercised in twos; if they are allowed to frolic up and down chasing and fighting with one another, they may well get into bad habits. However, they may be permitted to socialize with each other in a small enclosure or paddock.

At around six or seven months of age it can be good practice for the pup to chase a dummy hare or lure; this is easily done by putting a rabbit skin on a long piece of string and swinging it round and letting the pup chase it. Swinging it first clockwise and then anti-clockwise helps develop and strengthen the pup's limbs; it is also a good form of exercise.

Schooling with a Drag Hare

You may well want to run the pups behind a drag hare, if you have access to one. This is basically a large pulley or cog powered by a winder or battery, which reels in a soft toy on a long piece of thick string. If there is a soft toy attached to the drag then a squeaky toy can be put inside the soft toy – its squeaking helps stimulate the pups and makes them keener.

Three saplings enjoy the winter mud.

Before allowing the pup to chase the drag, let him play with the dummy hare – squeak it and tease him with it, throwing it close to him and letting him jump on it. Hopefully he should then be keen to chase the drag hare; in fact I have seen very few pups that won't chase a drag.

When the pups chase the dummy toy they will often pick it up and run around with it; this is instinctive, and it can be a good idea to let the pup have a little fun when he's caught his prey. However, make sure he doesn't get caught up in the wire.

If you have a pup that won't chase the drag hare, don't push him. Let him watch the other pups run, but don't let him have a go. Take him into a paddock with the dummy hare on a long piece of string and tease him with it – squeak the toy and roll it along the floor, or throw it and try and get the pup to chase it. If needs be, tie a blooded rabbit skin to the dummy and let him play with that.

When the pup is then put back behind the drag hare, you can use the same technique with the rabbit skin, and with any luck he should chase it. Always remember there is no

need to push the young pup: you can put him away for a few weeks before trying again.

I would also suggest that coursing a pup behind live prey is not the answer; if a pup is being schooled to chase a dummy hare, then showing him live quarry could have a derogatory effect on his development as a racer.

Schooling at the Track

Proper schooling at the track should not commence before a pup is twelve months old. For the first couple of times it is a good idea to take the pups to the track and just let them watch what's happening. You will often know straightaway which ones will go at the first attempt: while some go mad to get on the track, there will always be one or two that are busy looking around and quite oblivious to what's going on around them.

The first time the dog is allowed to run at the track the hare driver should be notified that it is a pup for schooling so he can drive the hare accordingly. He should be given a hand slip, starting 20 or 30 metres from the first bend; this will prevent him from getting

31

into full flight before he runs his first bend. If you're lucky he will chase all round the track but in fits and starts as he tries to negotiate these new surroundings. If he manages a full circuit you should be delighted, and as he completes the trip have your squeaky dummy hare handy to throw down for him. Let him have a minute to kill his toy as a reward for doing well.

If you are happy with the pup and he is a natural, then there is no rush; give him a week or two before giving him his second schooling trial.

After a couple of hand slips you may feel that he is ready to go into a trap, in which case I would suggest that the first couple of times you put him in you front load him: by this I mean put the pup rear first into the front of the trap, and then close it. Pups that are put in the normal way (through the back door) often get into the bad habit of turning in the racing box; this is because they try to get out the same way they have been put into the trap.

If you are lucky enough to have a trap at home, then you may already have the pup trap-trained. If so, it is useful to mask out the top of the lid so he has to get down and crouch to see out, because this teaches him to automatically assume the spring position when placed into a trap.

If all goes well, then give him a week to ten days between each of his next few runs; there is no need to rush a young dog. Furthermore, if he is chasing well at the schooling track, then you can rest him for a few weeks until he is fifteen months old and can start his grading trials.

Grading Trials

When a dog starts to have his grading trials at the race track you really want him to be as raw as possible. If he has had endless schooling trials he may well trial on at the race track much too fast. Ideally you want him to start to improve when he starts to race, so that with a bit of luck he can work his way through the card, winning several times in the process.

Two saplings out exercising.

If a pup is very gifted you may find that he grades in at the top of the card with little effort. Such a pup should be nurtured along and should not be run too frequently – in fact after a couple of races you may want to put him away for a couple of months and let him strengthen up. Sometimes young pups do not have sufficient muscular or mental strength, and having shown some initial potential, often benefit immensely from a 'maturing period': this is basically a break from racing for a month or two, in order to give them some time to mature.

Pups that don't chase can be a real problem: while some just take a little time to grasp what is required, others blatantly have no interest. For the latter I would advise enrolling them at a schooling track where they will be given a more in-depth education by professional trainers.

CHAPTER FOUR

Feeding

It is important for the greyhound that it is fed a balanced diet that meets the demands of a hard-working dog. While most feeds will provide in abundance what is required for a normal non-working dog, the greyhound requires something a little extra. To put it simply, you wouldn't put regular unleaded in a Formula 1 racing car. Indeed, the greyhound is unlike any other breed of dog, and if it doesn't receive the right amount of protein, carbohydrates, fats, vitamins and minerals, as described below, then its health and performance may well suffer.

THE ESSENTIAL CONSTITUENTS OF A BALANCED DIET

Protein: The building block of life; without it the body cannot survive. The body is in a constant form of change, and protein is continually being broken down to supply its needs. Protein is therefore needed to build and repair the greyhound's body, so it is important that it gets a good supply. The majority of protein will be supplied through meat, milk, eggs and fish, unless the dog is on a complete meal.

A young litter enjoy their morning meal.

Carbohydrates: The main heat and energy source for the greyhound; when it runs or exerts a lot of energy, it is the carbohydrates that are broken down and used as fuel. When the greyhound is in training, an abundance of carbs is required; however, when it is at rest, the extra carbs will become surplus to requirement and can easily be stored as body fat.

Fats: A secondary energy source that can be divided into two groups, animal fat and vegetable fat.

Vitamins and minerals: The racing greyhound is put under a very high level of physical and mental stress when racing. The importance of vitamins and minerals to help it cope with these stresses is often overlooked.

Vitamin A is important in preventing illness and infection; it is also essential for strong muscles and tendons, and a healthy coat.

Vitamin B1 is essential in the operation of the nervous system, and plays an important role in the breakdown of energy. Indeed, all the vitamins of the B complex are important to the health of the greyhound.

Vitamin C is also known as ascorbic acid, and helps in the removal of waste products from the muscles; it is required for healing wounds and broken bones, and is also a detoxicating agent.

Vitamin E is important in how efficiently oxygen is used throughout the body, and especially the muscles. It is also a natural antioxidant, which helps prevent the build-up of harmful compounds within the greyhound.

Calcium and *phosphorus* are essential for the growth and maintenance of the bones; however, these minerals are useless without the presence of *vitamin D*.

Electrolytes or *body salts* are an essential part of many of the dog's bodily functions. When the greyhound is in full training there comes a need for an increase in these body salts so the dog can cope with the stress that is placed on him.

Water

Water is essential to life, and its importance should never be taken lightly; if a dog becomes ill or has had a hard race, then the deprivation of water could be fatal. A large portion of the dog's bodyweight is actually made up from water, and when it exerts itself, a portion of this water is used up and needs to be replenished. All dogs should have water available to them on a twenty-four-hour basis; the only time this rule may be broken is on a race day. Some trainers like to take the water away after the morning feed to make sure the dog doesn't over-indulge on a hot day, because this could play havoc with the dog's race weight.

WAYS OF FEEDING

Complete Meal

In today's industry many trainers use a complete meal that can be both economical and much less hassle than the old-fashioned way of feeding. It is basically a dried meal that comes in a biscuit form, and it covers all the main dietary needs of the greyhound in one easy, ready-made meal that can save the trainer a lot of time and effort in food preparation. There are many different brands to choose from, and most have both a resting and a racing diet, the latter being generally much higher in protein. Most of these meals are made with the greyhound in mind, so it is generally the trainer's preference as to which he chooses to use.

Some trainers, however, still like to use the old-fashioned method of bread, meat and vegetables, or they use a combination of this and a complete meal, even though the old-fashioned methods are harder to organize, and involve a lot more messing about than using a complete meal. The advantage of using the old-fashioned method is that you have much more control over the dog's diet. For example, a dog's protein intake can be increased or decreased depending on the stage of training. I personally prefer to use a combination of the two methods.

The Old-Fashioned Method

Breakfast

Breakfast is the most important meal of the day, and it is essential for the dog that it constitutes a nutritious start. Once the dogs have been out for their morning walk and had their kennels cleaned out, then the breakfast ration can be given.

Mix powdered milk and warm water in a large tub; the ratio of powdered milk to water will probably differ between brands, but follow the instructions on the sack of milk powder.

For each greyhound give between two and five slices of brown bread, depending on the size of the dog and whether you are trying to put weight on the dog, or take it off.

Next add cornflakes: for the resting dog a handful on top of the bread is sufficient, and then add a scoop of milk. It is best to buy a big catering box of cornflakes from a wholesaler.

For the racing dog I would add a few goodies such as a tablespoon of glucose for energy, two raw eggs for protein, and a tot of sherry to warm a dog on a cold winter morning. The sherry may give a positive sample, so withdrawal prior to racing is important.

The Main Meal

First thing in the morning we light the boiler and make up a stew. The meat is usually horse meat, which you can buy legally from a slaughterhouse, though once or twice a week I would use turkey or fish, and we add a variety of vegetables; these include cabbage, swede, celery, carrots and a small onion. When the meat is cooked it is minced up with the vegetables and most of the broth used to soak a large tub of brown bread; a bit is left for gravy. A tub of raw meat can be minced as well to add to the feed of a few dogs. The bread is then mixed into a nice texture, not too runny, but not too thick either.

A tub of complete meal should be soaked: note that it is essential to use a lower protein meal if you are adding cooked or raw meat to the dog's ration.

To assemble the ration, put together a mixture of half bread and half meal, then add a little gravy and mix it up by hand. Then put a handful of meat and vegetables on the feed and add any supplements that the dog requires.

The size of the ration largely depends on the size of dog, and whether you need to build up the dog's weight or cut it down.

Lean or Heavy?

How much, and what, to feed can often be a question of trial and error, depending how much weight you want the dog to carry. I always prefer to have a good back on my dogs, but other trainers like to have their dogs lean. A good back should be when the hip and spinal bones are only just visible, though it is important that the dog is built up with muscle and not fat; this is achieved through constant hard work and good feeding. Some dogs are naturally lean, however, and because of this characteristic tendency a good solid back will never be achieved.

The trainer must also bear in mind that dogs will run better at different weights: thus some dogs run better when they are heavy, and others will not run well if they carry too much weight, so these dogs must be kept lean in order to achieve their best performance. It is only through trial and error that you will learn each dog's best race weight. Although it is not a hard and fast rule, I would suggest that a sprinter runs better with a good back, and a long-distance dog runs better when a little on the lean side. A sprinter is a dog that runs short distances of around 225 to 275m (250–300yds), and a long-distance dog runs anything over 540m (600yds); in between is known as a middle distance runner.

One of the benefits of the dog carrying a little extra weight is that if it gets run beyond its capability to recover, or if it becomes ill through sickness or disease, then it can cope much better with any substantial weight loss.

The most important thing to remember when feeding is to treat every dog as an individual. While one dog may hold its race weight with 'X' amount of food, another dog of a similar weight may well run off if you feed him the same amount.

SUPPLEMENTS

Supplements come in many and various forms from different companies, and it is the trainer's responsibility to decide which supplements will best suit which dogs.

Multi-vitamins: In my opinion it is essential to supplement a dog's ration with multi-vitamins in powder or tablet form. Whenever the greyhound races, its whole body, and primarily the organs and tissues, is subjected to immense stress. If it is not supplied with the correct nutrients the body will struggle to cope with the workload placed upon it, and the consequence is often poor or lack of consistent performance, and perhaps even breakdown or serious injury.

While the trainer may feel the dog is getting the correct amount of vitamins and minerals from its daily ration, it must be considered that their potency can be remarkably reduced through cooking, storage, processing and being exposed to heat or dampness.

Vitamin E: As a supplement, vitamin E can be very beneficial for nervous dogs, or dogs that suffer from muscle cramp or acidosis. The use of vitamin E can also help maximize racing performance, calm nervous dogs, encourage poor feeders to eat better, and aid recovery from race fatigue.

Electrolytes: These are important for any racing greyhound, but can particularly benefit the dog that is excitable, barks a lot, pants excessively, or is just a complete 'head case'. These dogs tend to 'run off', or struggle to hold their race form due to dehydration, because they use up a much higher percentage of their body salts than a well-behaved dog. The use of body salts can help the greyhound recover

more quickly from a race and prevent the onset of acidosis.

Kidney tonics: In a mild form these tonics can be used for a greyhound that struggles to urinate after they have raced, as they encourage it to drink more and therefore flush out the kidneys. This helps to prevent dehydration, and also helps the body clear the muscles of the acidic waste that can cause acidosis or cramp.

Creatine: This is a relatively new supplement, but one that has been used by human athletes for quite a few years. It is a compound produced naturally in our bodies as an energy replenisher, but supplementation can help increase energy levels and also act as a buffer for lactic acid.

DMG: Can be used to improve your greyhound's performance, but I prefer to use it as an anti-cramp supplement. While not every dog will respond well to it, some greyhounds will stop cramping as soon as they start taking it.

Cod liver oil: This supplement has been used for many years. It is derived from the liver of the cod fish, and has high levels of omega 3 fatty acids, vitamin A and vitamin D. Its health benefits include a healthy coat, nails and skin; it is also beneficial for easing the pain and joint stiffness associated with arthritis. I would give a splash of cod liver oil once or twice a week on the evening meal; overuse can lead to a build-up of toxins in the blood.

Ascorbic acid, or vitamin C: This supplement can be used daily to help reduce the onset of fatigue in the racing dog; I would give a 50mg tablet daily with the main meal.

Blood saturation dose: If I were preparing a dog for a certain race then I would give him what is known as a blood saturation dose the night before the race: 250mg for a small dog, and 300mg for a larger dog. The dose works not by helping to deliver more glycogen and oxygen to the muscles, but indirectly by helping the blood's transport system to stay clear for longer. I had a lot of success especially when supplementing dogs that were building up to fitness, and not necessarily on dogs that were fit already.

BAD EATERS

It is not unusual for a dog that comes into your care to go on hunger strike; most of the time it will only last a day or so, but occasionally you have a stubborn case. Such a dog is usually a new recruit that is nervous and often comes from a completely different environment, or it may be a dog that has had a serious illness. If the dog doesn't eat for several days then it can waste away quite quickly, so it is important to try and get some food into it.

I have never yet known a basically healthy dog turn up its nose at oily fish such as pilchards or sardines. By mixing the sardines into a bowl with a tin of rice pudding you create a smelly mixture that the dog usually finds irresistible. Once it starts to eat, then it is a case of gradually introducing your normal feed into its diet by mixing it a little at a time with the fish and rice pudding. After a week or so the dog should start to regain its appetite, and will hopefully soon eat its meals without any other such encouragement.

UPSET STOMACH

Occasionally a dog contracts a stomach complaint, or there may be a bout of kennel sickness going around, which has caused your dog's upset stomach; this is usually seen in dogs that have had symptoms of vomiting and diarrhoea. In this case a diet of rice and well-cooked chicken is a beneficial substitute to the dog's normal diet, which its stomach probably finds hard to cope with. You may well want to keep the dog on this diet for a good week, or until it is back to its normal self, and only then put it back on its regular diet.

GENERAL INFORMATION

- Always try and feed your greyhounds at the same time each day; the dog is a creature of habit and will know when meal time is.
- Don't give a very large feed to a thin dog; too much food at one time is likely to upset its stomach, causing diarrhoea. Give it three or four light meals instead.
- Never feed the meal too hot or too cold.
- Never feed your greyhound food that is old or that has been left out. You can usually smell the difference when food has gone off or sour, and it can turn very quickly in warm weather. Feeding food in this manner can seriously upset a dog's stomach, so it is really not worth the risk.
- If a dog is poorly don't leave food in with it in the hope that it eats something. If it turns its nose up at the food, remove it straightaway.
- Always keep food covered up to stop flies or any other parasite getting on the feed.
- If you use bread, make sure it is brown; don't use any bread with seeds on it as they may cause a positive test.

CHAPTER FIVE

The Training Routine and Race Preparation

Walking and galloping constitute an important part of any training routine, but are probably neglected to a certain degree by many trainers these days. Walking could be considered old fashioned, and trainers in the old days thought nothing of walking their dogs 8 to 10 miles a day. While this may seem somewhat extreme, it must be realized that the dogs were not subjected to the heavy workloads such as are put on them in today's racing industry.

Racing schedules have seen the amount of racing triple over the last couple of decades, and this has caused a change in the way that many dogs are trained, especially in the larger kennels. Thus it is not unusual for a dog to be expected to race twice a week or three times a fortnight, and this means the trainer has little opportunity to actually do any real training with his dogs. For me, this type of 'factory production line' racing, as seen at an ever-increasing number of tracks, is only beneficial to the financial backers of the tracks, people who often have little or no interest in what happens to the greyhounds when they are burned out or injured; the greyhounds are therefore often the ones that suffer, at the track's expense. Equally the trainers are under increasing pressure to produce a large number of dogs, and this trend means that it becomes much more difficult to train each dog as an individual: rather, they are trained in what may be called a 'collective' manner.

In my opinion this type of collective training is not what training a racing greyhound is all about. I was brought up into racing in the old-fashioned ways, and still believe that to get the very best out of each dog it must be treated as an individual; thus a sprinter should not be trained in the same way as a distance dog if you are to get the best out of him. Even so, regardless of the different types of dog you have in your kennel, walking on a daily basis should be a part of your routine.

There are many trainers who, for one reason or another, do very little walking with their dogs. Often the dogs are expected to exercise themselves in large paddocks, which is not always of benefit to them, because although some relish the freedom and will enthusiastically charge about until they are thoroughly leg-weary, others quite happily find a nice comfortable corner and just sit in the sun. For a dog that is resting or having a break from racing, this is an ideal way to let it down, but not if you want it racing fit.

It is important to realize that a dog cannot be kept in peak condition for more than eight to ten weeks before it will naturally have a dip in form. At this point it should be given a short break to reduce any risk of breakdown or burnout. By continuing to push the dog long after he is due a rest will encourage the risk of injury: dogs cannot be raced week in, week out, without unfortunate consequences.

A break of two to three weeks should be sufficient to let a dog recharge his batteries without a great loss in condition. When a dog is resting he should be doing just that: resting. He can then be put back into light work, and gradually built back up into top condition.

This type of training is known as 'cycling', and while the trainer needs to orchestrate the male dog's cycle, the greyhound bitch has her very own built-in cycle, namely the period of menstruation or coming in heat.

The combination of walking and galloping enables the trainer to condition his dog so they can be taken to peak fitness at just the right time. For the trainer with a lot of competition dogs, or one who likes a bit of a gamble, then this aspect of training needs to be taken to its limit. By training your dogs according to a routine that never changes from one day to another, you cannot hope to produce a dog in peak condition for any given race. However, you will almost certainly find that the dog will naturally produce its own cycle through sickness or injury: it is impossible for any dog to keep racing week in, week out, without any problems.

THE BENEFITS OF WALKING GREYHOUNDS

There are many benefits to walking your dogs if it is done in a structured way:

- You know how much exercise your dog is getting, and you can increase or decrease the workload depending on the individual dog. While a long-distance or marathon dog will improve with a strenuous workout, you will find that a short, stocky sprinter will not relish being walked mile after mile and thus his performance on the track will likely suffer.
- You can walk your dogs in different places; it is easy enough to put a few dogs in the back of the van and take them for a walk in a variety of alternative venues. Not only are there different things to see and smell, but going to a change of location is mentally stimulating for the dog. This alone can work wonders if you have a stale dog that has been stuck in the same routine week after week.
- Walking can give you and your dog a good cardiovascular workout. With a steady walk the dog's respiratory system and lungs can get a good workout without the strain on the heart and the nervous system that comes

from more intense activity. A good walking programme will also help to burn off any excess body fat.
- Greyhounds that have a good walking routine will have a much leaner and stronger physique. The walking undoubtedly helps with muscle tone, but it also helps loosen up stiff joints and muscles as the increased blood flow helps to flush out the chemical waste.
- Another benefit of walking is that you get a proper look at your dogs every day. A vital part of training is getting to know the individual dog's state of health, and a lot can be learned by checking its urine and faeces.

If you are running a large kennel it is a good idea to organize your dogs so they can be walked in sets of four or five. These sets should consist of dogs of similar standard: for example, you can put sprinters together, and lame dogs together, and so on. I would always walk in the morning and the afternoon, and then walk my specialist dogs again in the evening. On occasions I might get back from racing at midnight and coat up several dogs to take them out for a walk; if I was preparing a dog or two for certain races and felt they needed the work, then they would get it.

How Far and How Fast?

When walking it is good practice to start off slowly and then gradually increase the speed. It can improve the dog's fitness even further if you can work up to a slow trot. The distance you walk must be tailored to the needs of each individual.

Like any sort of exercise, walking must be structured according to the individual dog's expected workload. Thus a dog that is a marathon runner needs to develop its muscles and lungs to cope with the heavy burden that will be placed on them, while another that has to run a gruelling eight- or ten-bend race must be conditioned in such a fashion that its body's mechanics can cope with the task.

The majority of runners in a trainer's care are most likely to be four-bend dogs that don't need to be walked to the extent of long-

Express Ego, top Irish greyhound, leaving traps for a solo trial in preparation for the Greyhound Derby, Wimbledon Stadium, 26 April 2008. (© Steve Nash Photography)

distance dogs. However, a good 6 to 8km (4 or 5 miles) a day is a good starting point, and while this may seem quite far, in actual fact three twenty-minute walks a day at a decent pace will easily cover this distance.

Generally sprinters do not need the amount of walking each day that other dogs require. About 1.5km a day should be sufficient for a sprinter, as too much walking may well push the dog over the top and become counter-productive. A sprinter is an explosive runner and generally runs better without a great deal of work.

There are some important things to remember to do with walking.

- When taking on a new recruit, never walk them too much, too soon, as dogs that are not used to road work may well suffer from sore pads.
- Dogs should be built up gradually.
- Don't walk dogs too far when the temperature is high or the weather is very warm and sunny. Greyhounds can get heat stroke, and can dehydrate easily if they are not used to it.

GALLOPING

Bringing a dog into peak fitness for a certain competition or race can be manipulated by the trainer if he knows how to feed and exercise his dogs. Galloping should be considered one of the main aspects of training a greyhound, whether it is a track dog or a field dog. Like walking, however, galloping needs to be done in a structured way. Thus sprinters need to be galloped like sprinters, with short sharp gallops that can be anything from 50m to 300m, whereas greyhounds that run long-distance races will need a much more enduring galloping programme to help bring them into peak condition.

This should not be taken as a hard and fast rule, however; for example you may want to give your long-distance dog a series of short gallops to try and sharpen or freshen him up, or you may want to give a sprinter a series of longer gallops to help build his stamina. It is only with experience that you will learn for yourself what works best for you and your dogs.

Two greyhounds race hard across the gallop.

Galloping should be done in cycles, and how long a cycle lasts will largely depend on variables such as injuries, seasonal break, preparing for a competition, and how often dogs are rested. A typical cycle will start when a dog has come back from a rest or an injury, and the time it takes to get him back to full fitness will depend on how out of condition he is.

Before the dog returns to the track he should be given a couple of gallops to prepare him for his trial. Taking him back to the track after an injury with no preparation is asking for trouble, because the chances of injury, or an injury reoccurrence, are increased if he is run totally cold.

A dog that has suffered a serious injury may well benefit from a gallop into a bend before he has a trial. He should be taken 20 to 30m from the bend to prevent him getting anywhere near full flight before taking the turn.

Giving the dog a couple of pre-trial gallops also gives you the chance to take stock of his fitness, and any soreness or aggravation of an injury can be assessed without subjecting him to any serious piece of work. This could well save him from another lengthy lay-off if a bad injury flares up again because he was unprepared for the trial.

After the dog has had his first trial it may be that he will need one or two more trials before he is fit to run a race. If so, you can use these trials as fitness runs, with maybe just one gallop in between.

If the dog is straight on the card you can start to give him some serious work; how serious will depend on how quickly you want to bring him back to full fitness. If I were bringing a dog into condition I would have no qualms about galloping him twice a day, two days on, then one day off. The dog's fitness level, and the type of runner he was – sprinter or distance dog – would determine how far I galloped him. If a dog is worked hard he can be brought into good physical condition in a short space of time, providing he wasn't too out of shape to begin with.

It is quite possible to find a lot of race time with a dog if you get the timing of the races right. Thus if you were to leave the dog off the card for, say, three weeks, and then work him very hard with walking and galloping, you could feasibly find six to eight race lengths. Before returning to the track you may even wish to give him an unofficial trial at a different venue to establish how much he has improved.

When a greyhound has reached full fitness, the need to gallop him is minimized; also if the track expects him to run more than once a week, this in itself will keep him fit. However, I am a great believer in running a dog only once a week. Running twice a week occasionally will not cause too much distress, but do it on a frequent basis and you risk burnout or injury.

After a dog has reached full fitness he will only be able to sustain a top level of form for a couple of months. Thus when he starts to dip in form it can be a good idea to give him a short break; he can be put on light duties for anywhere up to a month to recharge his batteries.

A new cycle can then begin, and you can gradually work him back to full fitness.

Pre- and Post-Race Galloping

The day before a race a gallop is a complete 'no' for me: dogs should be totally rested then, with exercise cut down to the bare minimum – a couple of short walks to loosen themselves up and to relieve themselves.

Likewise the day after a race should be a nice relaxing day. While some dogs will bounce back from a race relatively quickly, others may need a day or two to recover. It is for the trainer to judge whether a dog will need a gallop before its next run, and how soon after a race he thinks it can cope.

Race-Day Gallop

A gallop on the morning of the race can be beneficial to many greyhounds. I am not talking about a 500m, full-on gallop, but a short 100m gallop before breakfast followed by a good massage can work wonders on a race day. In particular, dogs that cramp up in a race seem to benefit immensely from a race-day gallop, and it is an option that shouldn't be ruled out.

RACE PREPARATION

Race preparation will vary a lot between each dog. Here I have put together a basic seven-day pre-race preparation that I would use when bringing a dog to fitness. This is quite an aggressive week's work, and one that would be trimmed down each week as the dog reached full fitness. Also the length and frequency of the gallops would be tailored to the individual dog.

I would advise that you experiment with each dog as to how much or how little work it needs in order to get the best from it: thus while some dogs thrive on hard work, give others a lot and they will leave their race at home.

Day One

- Let the dog out to relieve himself, and give him a brisk walk for about a mile.
- Before breakfast give him a gallop, massage him down afterwards, and then give him his breakfast.
- Breakfast would consist of milk, two slices of wholemeal bread, cornflakes, two tablespoonfuls of glucose powder and two raw eggs.
- Around mid-morning check him over for injury, groom and massage him, and finally wash off his feet.
- In the early afternoon walk him again for a mile and a half, and then bring him back and give him another short gallop and massage him down.
- Give him a couple of hours' rest and then feed the main meal.
- The main meal would consist of brown bread, race meal, meat and vegetables, and a supplement of multi-vitamins and 50mg of ascorbic acid.
- Allow him to relieve himself, then put him back to bed.
- Late evening give him another brisk walk of a couple of miles, massage him down, and coat him up ready to be put to bed.

Day Two

- Let the dog out to relieve himself, and give him a brisk walk for about a mile.
- Before breakfast give him a gallop, massage him down, then give him his breakfast.
- Breakfast would consist of milk, two slices of wholemeal bread, cornflakes, two tablespoonfuls of glucose powder and two raw eggs.
- Around mid-morning check the dog over, groom and massage him, and wash off his feet.
- Early afternoon walk him again for a mile and a half, then give him another short gallop and afterwards massage him down.
- Give him a couple of hours rest, then feed the main meal.
- The main meal would consist of brown bread, race meal, meat and vegetables, and

a supplement of multi-vitamins and 50mg of ascorbic acid.
- Allow the dog to relieve himself, and put him back to bed.
- In the late evening give him another brisk walk of a couple of miles, massage him down, coat him up and put him to bed.

Day Three (Rest Day)

- Let the dog out to relieve himself, and give him a brisk walk for about a mile.
- Breakfast should consist of milk, two slices of wholemeal bread, cornflakes, two tablespoonfuls of glucose powder and two raw eggs.
- Around mid-morning check the dog over, groom and massage him, and wash off his feet.
- In the early afternoon walk him again for a mile and a half, then bring him back and give him another short gallop and massage him down.
- Give him a couple of hours rest, then feed the main meal.
- The main meal would consist of brown bread, race meal, meat and vegetables, and a supplement of multi-vitamins and 50mg of ascorbic acid.
- Allow him to relieve himself, and put him back to bed.
- In late evening give him another brisk walk of a couple of miles, massage him down, coat him up and put him to bed.

Day Four

- Let the dog out to relieve himself, and give him a brisk walk for about a mile.
- Before breakfast give him a gallop, massage him down, and then give him his breakfast.
- Breakfast would consist of milk, two slices of wholemeal bread, cornflakes, two tablespoonfuls of glucose powder and two raw eggs.
- Around mid-morning check the dog over, groom and massage him, and wash off his feet.
- In the early afternoon walk him again for a mile and a half, bring him back and give him another short gallop, and massage him down.

- Give him a couple of hours rest, then feed the main meal.
- The main meal would consist of brown bread, race meal, meat and vegetables, and a supplement of multi-vitamins and a 50mg tablet of ascorbic acid.
- Allow him to empty, and put him back to bed.
- In the late evening give him another brisk walk of a couple of miles, massage him down, coat him up and put him to bed.

Day Five

- Let the dog out for an empty, and give him a brisk walk for about a mile.
- Before breakfast give him a gallop, massage him down and then give him his breakfast.

- Breakfast would consist of milk, two slices of wholemeal bread, cornflakes, two tablespoonfuls of glucose powder and two raw eggs.
- Around mid-morning check him over, groom and massage him, and wash off his feet.
- In the early afternoon walk him again for a mile and a half, then bring him back and give him another short gallop and massage him down.
- Give him a couple of hours rest, then feed the main meal.
- The main meal would consist of brown bread, race meal, meat and vegetables, and a supplement of multi-vitamins and a 50mg tablet of ascorbic acid.
- Allow him to empty himself, and put him back to bed.
- Late evening give him another brisk walk of

Farloe Theleader leaves Trap 5 (2nd from left) on the way to victory at Monmore Stadium, Wolverhampton on 9 March 2007. (© Steve Nash Photography)

a couple of miles, massage him down, coat him up and put him to bed.

Race Day Eve

- The day before the race should be a complete rest day.
- Breakfast would consist of milk, two slices of wholemeal bread, cornflakes, two tablespoonfuls of glucose powder and two raw eggs.
- Massage the dog mid-morning, and let him out to relieve himself a couple of times during the day.
- The main meal would consist of brown bread, race meal, meat and vegetables, and a supplement of multi-vitamins.
- Allow him out to empty himself, then put him to bed.
- Around 9 o'clock take the dog to relieve himself, and give him a small bed-time meal. This would consist of a slice of bread and a small amount of cornflakes mixed with a little milk, and a blood saturation dose of ascorbic acid; add an optional tot of sherry to this meal.
- The dog should then be coated up and put to bed.

Race Day

- Race day should start with a short walk to let the dog have an empty. Give him a short ten-minute massage before coating him up and giving him breakfast.
- Breakfast should consist of milk, two slices of wholemeal bread, cornflakes, two tablespoonfuls of glucose powder and two raw eggs.
- Leave him to rest for the morning; if he is racing in the evening give him a short walk to relieve himself.
- When he is taken out of his kennel for the race, massage him down and if possible give him a trot around to try and get some blood flowing into the muscles. This will help him warm himself up and will prepare his muscles for the task at hand.

POST RACE

After the race has finished and you collect the dog at the trip it is good practice to quickly check him over by eye. As you walk him off, give him a bit of lead and just watch his general breathing and how he moves; let him walk back at his own pace.

After this, clean him off, wash his feet and give him a general check over. It is important to give him a breather before you put him away; walking him round for a few minutes after the race will help remove any waste products from his muscles. This cooling off period will also help him catch his tongue a little before he is put back in the race kennel.

If he is in the last race it is important to let him catch his tongue and give him time to recover from any heavy panting before he is transported home. In hot weather this is even more important, as he would be at serious risk of heat stroke.

When the greyhound gets home he should be given a chance to relieve himself before putting him back in his kennel. He should have fresh clean water available at all times, but after a race electrolytes should be added to help replace any lost body salts.

Any injuries should be treated and any wounds cleaned up before the dog is given his final meal of the day. Treating injuries at an early stage can be very beneficial to the satisfactory outcome and prognosis of the injury. He can then be fed, coated up and put to bed.

The Day After a Race

The day after the race most dogs should be given light duties; the older dog is likely to suffer more than the young dog, as is the long-distance dog. However, it is still important that he is given two or three short walks to help stimulate the muscles and flush them out. Massaging and magnetic field therapy treatment can also greatly aid in the dog's recovery; these areas are discussed in more depth in Chapter 11.

CHAPTER SIX

The Anatomy
of the Greyhound

I would consider it fairly important that the novice handler has at least a basic knowledge of the greyhound's anatomy. While it is not imperative that you become an expert, it can help with a lot of problems if you have some idea about what's going on.

THE SKELETAL SYSTEM

The greyhound's body consists of approximately 321 bones of various shapes and sizes. They are generally split into two groups.

Firstly there are the long bones, the short bones and the sesamoid bones, which are found in the dog's limbs. The short bones are exclusive to the wrist and hock, and both consist of seven in number. The femur or tibia of the hind limb or the radius and ulna in the forelimb are good examples of long bones. The sesamoid bones are located around free-moving joints and have three important functions: they protect the tendons as they pass over bony surfaces, they increase the surface area for the attachment of the tendons, and they direct the passage of the tendon across the joint.

Secondly there are the flat bones and the irregular bones that are found in the skull and the vertebral column. Flat bones are found in the skull, where they surround and shield the brain. The irregular bones belong to the spine and are also found in the skull.

The skeleton has four main functions:

• It supports the body and also protects its vital organs.

• The bones act as levers for the muscular system and the dog's movement.
• The bones themselves are actual living tissue that needs a supply of vital minerals (calcium and phosphorus); this is supplied through the blood. These minerals keep the bones healthy and also supply other parts of the body.
• The bones have a role in how the red and white blood cells work.

The Joints
A joint is when two or more bones come together and are joined by a strong elastic tissue known as a ligament. The most important joint is known as a synovial joint; it is characterized by the joint capsule. Within the joint capsule lies a synovial membrane that covers all the structures within the joint. It secretes a fluid known as synovial fluid, which has three main functions:

• It helps the bones slide effortlessly over each other; they are sprung apart by the fluid, but are held in place by the natural pressure of the ligaments and surrounding tissue. When damage occurs to any of the supporting ligaments the whole joint becomes compromised.
• It supplies the joint with vital nutrients.
• It disposes of waste products within the joint.

The fluid within the joint is of paramount importance to the health of that joint. If the flow of the fluid slows down, then bone ends and

46

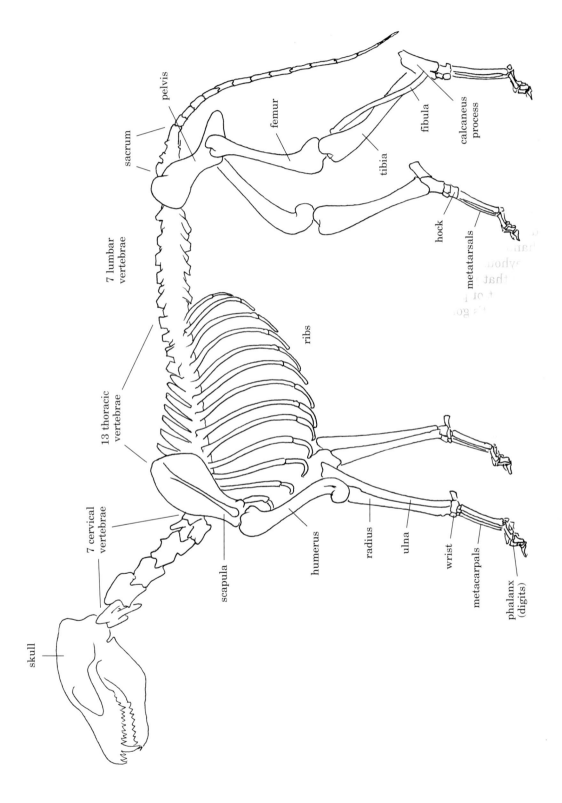

The skeleton of the greyhound.

skull

7 cervical vertebrae

scapula

humerus

radius

ulna

wrist

metacarpals

phalanx (digits)

7 lumbar vertebrae

13 thoracic vertebrae

ribs

pelvis

sacrum

femur

tibia

fibula

calcaneus process

hock

metatarsals

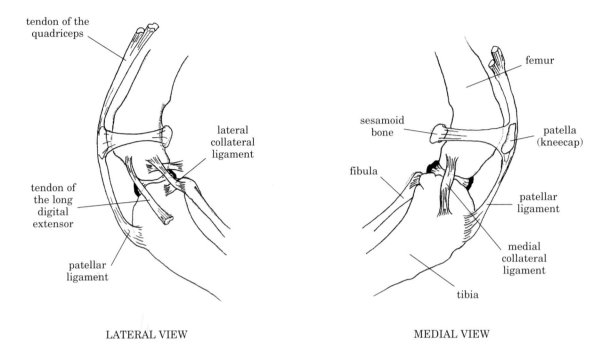

LATERAL VIEW · MEDIAL VIEW

Both sides of the knee joint and the series of ligaments that sustain the joint.

cartilage become brittle and the surrounding soft tissue dries out and loses its stretchiness.

THE MUSCLES

The dog's muscles provide many functions throughout the body; primarily they are the locomotive power of the limbs and joints, but they are also involved in the circulation and respiration. The muscle fibres are split into three classifications: smooth muscle, cardiac muscle and skeletal muscle.

- Smooth muscle fibres are found in the organs and the blood vessels, and are associated with the glands and the spleen.
- The cardiac muscle fibres are those of the heart.
- The skeletal muscle fibres are found in the muscles that provide the dog's locomotive power.

For the trainer it is the skeletal muscles that

are of great importance because of the damage that can be sustained by them. Not only does he need to learn about the injuries they might sustain, he also needs to learn how they can be managed to help prevent and repair injuries.

A more in-depth look at muscles, joints and bones is provided in Chapter 9, concerning racing injuries, and in Chapter 11 we take a closer look at injury prevention and repair.

THE HEART

The heart is basically a pump that directs the blood through the arteries and the veins; the arteries carry blood away from the heart, while the veins bring the blood back. The heart is a cone-shaped organ roughly the size of a clenched fist; the male heart is always bigger than the female heart.

The heart's left side takes in the oxygenated blood from the lungs and disperses it through the body tissue, and the right side takes in the

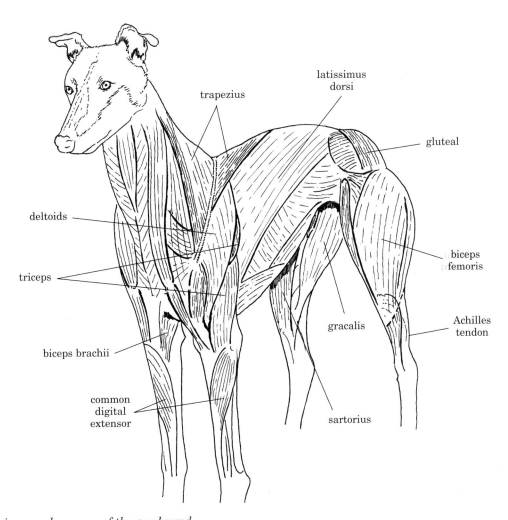

The major muscle groups of the greyhound.

blood from the tissue and sends it back to the lungs to be re-oxygenated and to disperse any waste products.

When the greyhound runs or is worked hard, the heart beats much faster to supply the muscles with blood. While the heart has its own natural beating rhythm the strength and number of beats is coordinated by the brain and the nervous system.

The number of times the heart pumps is known as the heart rate, and can be monitored at certain points where it passes along the arteries: this is known as the pulse.

Any problem in the heart has an immediate effect on the supply of oxygen to the body and how it disperses it. This can be critical to how a greyhound performs, so any problems need to be investigated by your veterinarian.

THE BLOOD

The blood consists of red blood cells, white blood cells and plasma:

• Red blood cells are used to carry oxygen from the lungs to the rest of the body.

- White blood cells are the basis of the immune system, and protect the body from infection and from any invasion of bacteria and viruses.
- Plasma consists of many products such as nutrients, electrolytes and waste products, but its main constituent is water.

The greyhound has about 3 litres of blood in circulation around its body. Blood has many functions, including the supply of fluids to the body, the control of body temperature and the regulation of hormones. If the dog has any severe loss of blood then it cannot survive.

THE LUNGS

The lungs are the main organ of the respiratory system and their purpose is to transport oxygen to the greyhound's body through the blood. Air (oxygen) is taken in through the nose and mouth and delivered to the lungs through the windpipe. The oxygen is dispersed into the blood through the lungs, and carbon dioxide is taken out of the blood in the lungs and disposed of through the mouth and nose. It is primarily the function of oxygen to break down food for the body to use as fuel or energy, and it is this energy that maintains the life and health of the dog.

It is the brain's task to regulate the rate of breathing and the amount of oxygen and carbon dioxide that are within the dog's system. When the greyhound races he has a much greater requirement for energy, and the respiratory system must work overtime as the dog quickly takes air in and out of the lungs. By gradually building up the greyhound's training and exercise programme the respiratory system can be strengthened. Through walking and galloping the lungs' capacity can be heightened or improved so the dog can ultimately increase its performance capability.

THE NERVOUS SYSTEM

The brain is the information box that gives and receives information; it does this via the

nerves. The nerves respond to the dog's environment and send messages via the spinal cord to the brain. It is the nervous system that looks after and regulates all the dog's bodily organs and functions: this could be anything from its heart rate or breathing to when it is hungry or needs a drink.

It is important to understand that proper functioning of the greyhound's nervous system is critical to its health and well-being. For example, when it comes out of its kennel at the race track it can see, smell and hear its surroundings, and its bodily functions automatically

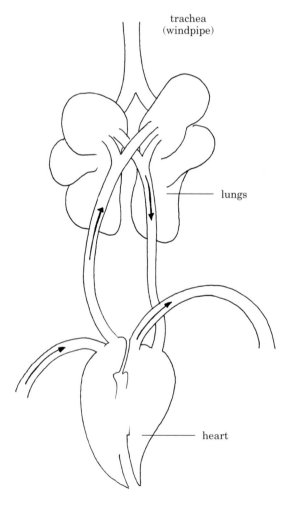

The heart and the lungs, showing the direction of the flow of blood.

respond to what its brain perceives of the situation. Thus the heart rate may elevate, the dog may jump about in excitement, and it may start to bark in anticipation of the race: these are all responses of the nervous system.

Another example would be that when the dog races, it is the brain that initiates how the limbs move to propel the dog forwards. The limbs, heart rate and breathing are automatically regulated by the nervous system.

It must also be understood by the greyhound handler that it is the nervous system that responds to stress. When the dog becomes cold it shivers, when it becomes hot it pants heavily. As a handler you can help the dog compromise a stressful situation – for example you can put a coat on it if it is cold, or you can open a window or put on a fan to try and keep it cool.

THE IMMUNE SYSTEM

The greyhound must take in oxygen and also consume food for its survival, but within the air and within the food and water chain are lurking parasites, bacteria, fungi and other nasty viruses. It is the immune system that defends the greyhound's body from foreign invaders and infection. The backbone of the immune system is the white blood cells that travel around in the blood and enter the body's tissue. Their job is to patrol the body in search of any foreign invaders or materials. The white blood cells then produce antibodies to kill any foreign invaders, and alert the rest of the body to their presence.

As well as the white blood cells the dog has more cavalry at hand; thus within the stomach, for example, lies acid that will destroy any materials that have managed to avoid the saliva and the hairs within the lungs. Also tear drops are produced by the eye to flush out any foreign invaders. Without the immune system any minor infection could be fatal to the dog.

It is through vaccinations that the immune system is built up to protect the body from invasion.

THE URINARY SYSTEM

The kidney is a vital organ that filters the waste products from the blood and looks after the fluid levels within the greyhound's body. Blood is transported into the kidneys via the renal artery and taken away by the renal vein. When in the kidney the blood is filtered, and the waste products, known as urine, are then transported into the bladder and disposed of when the dog urinates.

Some trainers or handlers like to use a dipstick test on a regular basis to check the dog's urine. In this test a short strip of card with several colours on it is dipped into a bowl of the dog's urine and then matched against the colour chart provided. This test can provide the trainer with useful information regarding any problems in the kidneys and urinary system, such as minor infections and inflammations. If a dog is underperforming for no apparent reason a urine test can be a good starting point if it is not suffering any obvious injury.

CHAPTER SEVEN

General Care
of the Greyhound

It will largely depend on the number of dogs in your care as to how much time you can spend on each dog on a daily or weekly basis. If possible it is important that each dog is given some sort of personal attention every day, even if only a quick brush-over. Greyhounds are like any other breed of dog in the sense that they relish human attention, and thrive on one-to-one care.

CARE OF THE TEETH

The teeth of the greyhound need plenty of attention due to the way it is fed. The soft or moist diet that is fed by the majority of trainers leaves the teeth susceptible to tartar build-up and possible gum infection. Tartar is a hard substance that forms around the teeth and comes from bacteria in the mouth, and from general food matter. When the teeth are left unattended or untreated, then problems with the teeth and gums are inevitable; infection or deterioration of the gums and rotten teeth are the most common problems. However, if bacteria get into the blood, this could lead to a much more serious infection.

For the racing dog, bad teeth can be a real problem due to the detrimental effect this can have on its performance. I have seen greyhounds improve many lengths after they have had the bad teeth taken out and their gums treated.

While some greyhounds have good, strong, healthy teeth, others will develop problems even if you care for them on a daily basis.

Some dogs seem to suffer with bad breath, tartar build-up and gum problems even if you clean them regularly. If the handler can clean them every day, then at least the problem can be minimized.

For care of the teeth you need a toothbrush, a tooth scraper and a small metal tub. There are different toothpastes available, but I have always used a small tub of water with a dash of hydrogen peroxide in it.

Start off by giving the teeth a quick brush and a general check over, looking out for any signs of rot, and the degree of tartar build-up; the latter could be anything from a soft brown coating that scrapes off easily, to a rock-hard substance that really takes some shifting.

To scrape the dog's right side, place the left hand round its muzzle with your index finger between the teeth. With the scraper in your right hand, lift the gum and start to remove the tartar. Try to work across the tooth to begin with, and work up to the gum. It is inevitable that you will catch the gum at some point and make it bleed, however, be as careful as you possibly can to avoid doing so. If the tartar is bad you may need to use quite a bit of force to remove it, and for these cases you will probably have to come in from the top and pull down with the scraper.

If you are right-handed you may find it rather more difficult to scrape the teeth on the left side. Try standing to the dog's side, and use your left hand to press its muzzle in to your legs and to hold back its lip while you scrape the teeth. If the dog has a serious build-up of

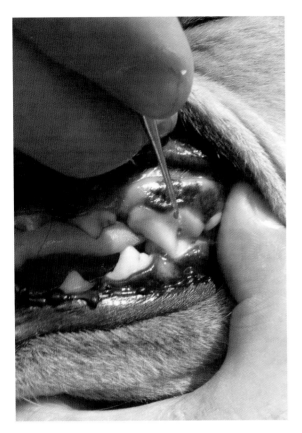
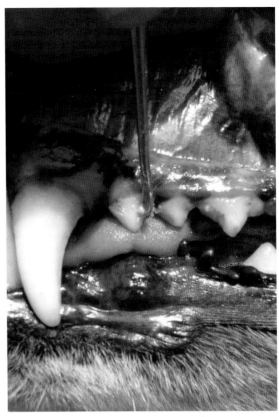

It is important to use the scaler in the correct manner to remove the tartar and to reduce the chance of damage to the gums whilst scraping.

After the scraping is complete, brush the teeth with a toothbrush; water, or water with a drop of hydrogen peroxide, can be used to clean the teeth and rinse the mouth.

tartar then it is much easier to remove just the worst of it first, and then get a bit more off each day or every other day until the teeth are free of it.

Some dogs will greatly resist you when you scrape their teeth, and in this case you may need to straddle the dog and back his rear end into a corner; this will stop him backing away underneath you as you are trying to work. Inevitably this will make the job a little more difficult, but should not hinder you too much. However, it is important that if a dog is getting upset you should not push him too much, and never get heavy-handed with him as this will only make the job harder. If he is getting too distressed, put him back in his kennel and try again in a couple of days' time, and just do a little bit at a time.

Giving knuckle bones or other chewable materials can be a great help in combating tartar build-up and the removal of tooth debris. Bones should be of the large beef knuckle-bone variety, and should be well cooked. When a bone is given in a kennel the dog's bedding should be removed to prevent it swallowing any unwanted materials.

After the dog has chewed the bone, the task of cleaning the teeth should be easier.

CARE OF THE EARS

The greyhound's ears should be checked and cleaned every week. They can be cleaned out with cotton wool or a cotton bud to remove any build-up of wax, and should be checked for any damage, injury or infection. When a dog is

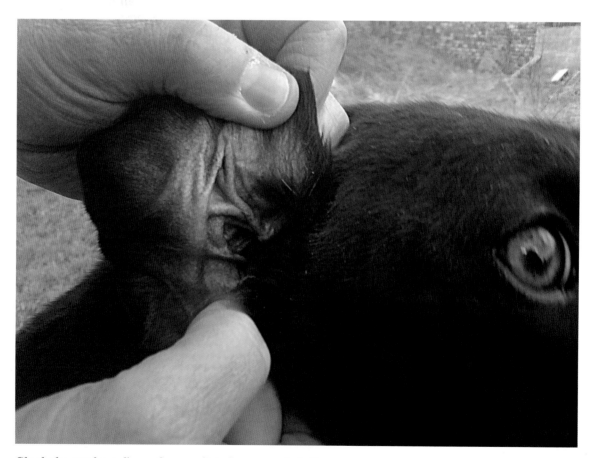

Check the greyhound's ear for any dirt, damage or infection.

experiencing pain within the ear it will hold its head on one side or will frequently shake its head.

It is not uncommon for dogs to get a soft swelling on the ear flap; this could be anything up to the size of an egg, and may be purple in colour. Such an injury is quite often sustained from a serious knock or blow to the head, and is the result of a damaged blood vessel. The ear will undoubtedly be very painful.

It can be beneficial to use a warm kaolin poultice on the ear every six to eight hours to reduce the swelling. If there is no response then the handler will need to call a veterinarian, who will drain the ear and prescribe the best course of treatment.

Infection or inflammation of the ear, often known as canker, is usually the result of negligence. Ears that are left unattended and are not cleaned out will usually develop an ear problem of some description. Dirt or ear mite infestations are two common problems that affect the greyhound – or indeed any dog – and it is important that the ears are cleaned out and treated. They should be carefully cleaned with a small cotton-wool ball soaked in a 50/50 mixture of water and TCP; the ball should be squeezed dry before cleaning commences. Use the cotton wool to remove any dirt, but take great care not to go deep into the ear, or to press too hard and aggravate the ear further.

If ear mites are present they can usually be seen through a magnifying glass; they are small and white in appearance, and they live on the brown wax. It is important to clean all the dirt away with soapy water, then cleanse the area with a TCP solution on a cotton bud. Ear drops that have been prescribed from the vet often need to be used.

Any serious or chronic cases of ear infection or inflammation should be presented to a veterinarian to determine the exact cause of the problem. A deep ear infection can sometimes be linked with a throat infection, but whatever the cause, it will need more aggressive therapy than the handler is qualified to deliver, and the vet must be called.

GROOMING

Grooming is a vital part of your one-on-one time with your greyhound. Most greyhounds love to be combed and brushed, but I believe that it is that individual attention that the dog craves.

Your equipment should consist of a good horse brush, a flea comb, a hacksaw blade, two good grooming gloves and a clean towel. Always start by giving the dog a good brush over, to remove any dirt or muck from the coat or lower legs. The brush should have fairly hard bristles and should be used quite firmly in a back-and-forth motion.

The hacksaw blade is used to remove any dead hair; this implement is cheap, and just as effective as any purpose-made coat-removing brush or comb that you can buy. When using the hacksaw, just run the blade smoothly in the direction the coat lies; this is generally

The stiff brush is a useful tool for removing any dry dirt out of the coat.

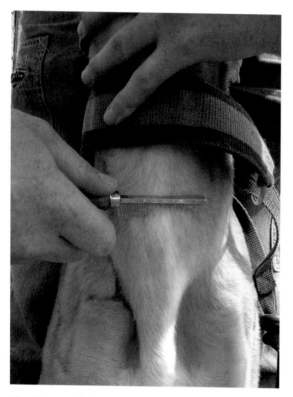

The flea comb is used to remove any unwanted passengers that the greyhound has picked up.

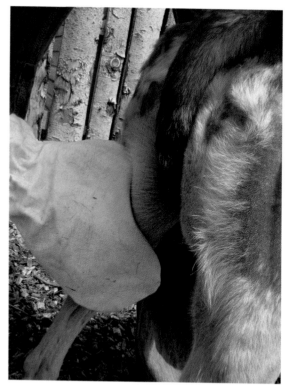

The grooming glove is used to massage down and brush off the coat.

head to tail and horizontally – never work against the lie of the dog's coat. It is important not to use the blade too firmly because you may damage the skin, and also not for too long a time. If you have a puppy that is very woolly, then do just a little every day until the adult coat starts to come through.

Next, use the flea comb to check for any unwanted passengers: the top of the neck, the chest, the top of the tail and between the legs are the most common areas to find these persistent little parasites. A useful way to dispose of them is in a bucket of water that you keep at hand to drop them in; if you try to kill them on the comb, you always end up losing some.

Then put a grooming glove over each hand, and using a circular motion, work over the whole of the dog: start with the neck, then work down the shoulders and across the back, and finish off down the hind legs.

Finally, take a towel and give him a good rub over for several minutes, then run the towel the length of his back several times.

The Feet and Nails

The feet or paws should be washed on a daily basis to clean out any debris, especially from around the quick area and the base of the nail. Fill a bucket with warm, soapy water, then wash the feet thoroughly and inspect them for any damage.

Some trainers like to clip their dog's nails, but I prefer to file them. It is important to keep the nails fairly short to reduce the risk of injury: the nails should not touch the floor when the dog is standing on a hard, even surface.

When a greyhound has an injured toe it is possible to file a nail back extremely short to relieve the pressure on it. While it may take a few weeks to bring the quick back, I think it is

Filing a greyhound's nails is not a task that will come easily, especially to the novice handler. However, with perseverance and practice it is a job that is beneficial to both handler and dog. It is highly unlikely that you will ever make a nail bleed, and the dog is usually a lot more comfortable with the handler filing than with the clip, clip, clip of the clippers.

far better for the dog than just chopping off a full nail.

When examining the nails you will see a pink sleeve of blood within the nail: this is known as the 'quick', and it should not be damaged when the nail is cut.

Dogs that have had a bad experience from having their nails cut are often reluctant to have them cut again. Certainly when using clippers it can be very difficult not to damage the quick, which is why my preference is to use a file.

Dogs that have very long nails usually have a long quick, though if the nails are filed regularly it is possible to bring the quick back, thus enabling the trainer to get the greyhound's nails a lot shorter.

Standing over the dog and facing its rear, lift the foot off the floor, then separate each toe and work away with the file for five or six strokes before bringing a stroke back. As you file, when you get close to the quick the nail will feel soft so you can stop filing.

At first it will feel clumsy and awkward to use a file, but with perseverance you will be able to shape the nails nicely. Dogs that protest at having their nails clipped will often stand quietly while you file them.

Clipping the greyhound's nails should be done with extreme care. Clipping the quick and making the nail bleed can often lead to distress and discomfort.

It is sometimes essential to clip the nails when they have got too long. It is important to try not to clip the pink quick, because this is what bleeds and often causes the dog distress. Dogs that have been butchered by an inexperienced handler usually end up very nervous about having their nails cut.

When a greyhound has long nails it is better to use the clippers first, but to clip well away from the quick, and then use the file to take the nail a little shorter. The nails can be filed down over several sessions, and don't have to be taken back short enough straightaway.

If a nail is clipped too tight and is bleeding badly, a little potassium permanganate can be put on some cotton wool and held to the nail to stop the bleeding.

PARASITES AND SKIN PROBLEMS

The Flea

The flea can be a major problem for the trainer, especially in the summer months. The flea is a blood-sucking parasite that has troubled the dog since time began, and finds the greyhound to be a good host. Due to the greyhound's lifestyle the flea seems to have little trouble in infesting all the dogs in your kennels if you don't get on top of the problem quickly.

Most commonly the greyhound will pick up fleas out in grassy fields or paddocks, but obviously when he goes to the race track he interacts with dogs from other kennels, and sleeps in a kennel that may have been used by several other dogs in the previous week.

In my experience certain dogs seem to be more prone to flea infestation than others; for example, you sometimes have two dogs in a kennel, and only one of them will have fleas and the other will be clean. This could be attributable to either the type or the temperature of the blood.

The flea is a secondary host to the tapeworm, and they have formed an inter-dependent life cycle. Thus the flea larvae eat tapeworm eggs, which then develop into cysts inside the flea; these remain dormant until the adult flea bites the dog, which, irritated, in turn bites at the affected area of its skin. In doing so it swallows the flea, and the cysts within the flea then develop into adult worms within the dog's gut. Segments of the worms pass through the dog in its faeces: the segments are full of eggs, which are deposited in the environment and the cycle starts again.

The female flea will feed on the dog before jumping off into some small, hidden crack

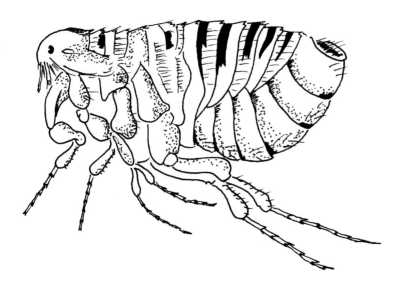

The flea is a parasitic scourge of all dogs, including the greyhound.

within the kennel to lay its eggs, which hatch out when the weather gets warmer. These hatchlings develop into adult fleas, which jump on to the nearest dog to find a meal. After the flea has had its fill it deposits vomit and faecal matter, identified as small red-brown particles, into the dog's coat.

It is important to check each dog regularly for fleas, as they can cause many levels of skin problem. Furthermore, when treating the dog for fleas it is important that the kennel is treated at the same time. The dog should be bathed in shampoo designed to kill the fleas, and it should be bathed completely, making sure you get around its private parts, behind the ears, around the chest and down the forelegs and feet. While the dog is being bathed the kennel should be stripped and scrubbed, and all bedding burned. The kennel – including the walls, floor, door and bed – should then be treated with a flea powder or spray.

Subsequently the dog's coat should be combed through with a flea comb on a daily basis to reduce the risk of reinfestation.

The Sheep Tick

The sheep tick is another parasite that likes a good feed on your greyhounds now and again. It attaches itself to the dog with its sharp teeth, and as it fills with blood, looks increasingly like a big blue wart; if you try to pull it off, there is a good chance you will leave a nasty wound on the dog. The best way to remove a tick is to use a pair of special tweezers that you heat up; you then grab hold of the tick with the tweezers and hopefully it will let go of the dog. It should then be destroyed to prevent it finding a new host.

Worms

The tapeworm is the worm that most commonly infests the greyhound; it is long and thin and is made up of many tiny, incomplete segments. The worm sits in the gut and feeds on the nutrients that you feed to your dog every day. It can infest the greyhound through the food chain (raw meat), or by biting at or swallowing infected fleas.

As the worm grows and develops in the gut of the host, some of the tiny segments will break off and be deposited in the faeces. It is here in the fields or paddocks that other animals, including fleas, swallow the eggs; the eggs get into the bloodstream of the flea and become a bloodworm, where they stay dormant until they reach the gut of a new host.

Common signs of tapeworm infestation are segments of the worm around the anus, and the dog can often be seen dragging its bum across the floor or bed. Its coat can appear dull and out of condition, and it may well start running up and losing condition over its back. You may also find that you struggle to get weight on a lean dog that definitely should be holding more condition than it is.

Treatment consists of a good wormer to clear the tapeworm out of the gut; these can be obtained from your veterinarian. The removal of any fleas is a crucial part of the treatment as the majority of tapeworm infestations will come from fleas. It is usually advisable to worm your dog once every six months as a precautionary measure.

The roundworm is a parasite that very rarely infests the adult greyhound. However, it is usually seen in puppies and can be dangerous to the young animal. Roundworms are covered more thoroughly in Chapter 3 (*see* page 29).

Ringworm

Ringworm is not in fact a worm, but a parasitic fungus that invades the skin and hair roots; it is extremely contagious. The hair falls out in small, circular patches, leaving the skin bald: hence the name 'ringworm' – though depending on where the fungus takes hold, the bald areas are not always circular in shape. The ringworm may form in more that one location on the dog's body, and can often be found on the head.

To deal with ringworm, first cut away the hair around the circular areas and clean them with surgical spirit. Apply tincture of iodine every day for about a week, and then on alternate days for another week. Because the fungus is so contagious it is advisable to wear disposable gloves when treating ringworm.

Dandruff

Dandruff can sometimes be a problem for the greyhound; it always looks worse on a black dog. Surgical spirit can be worked into the coat and rubbed back against the run of the hair to bring the dandruff out; it can then be brushed off.

A tablespoon of cod liver oil can be placed on the dog's dinner three times a week to help improve the coat and skin.

BILING OUT

Biling out, or inducing your greyhound to be sick, may seem a barbaric practice to the novice handler. However, it can greatly improve the dog's health, and certainly improves the performance of the racing dog. Greyhounds that have thick saliva around the mouth after a race will often benefit the most from 'biling out'.

Bile is formed in the liver and is then released into the intestine to help in the absorption of fat molecules into the body. It is believed that due to the low fat diet of the greyhound, bile is not released to the levels that it should be, and an accumulation of bile forms in the liver.

When the greyhound is vigorously exercised, bile and saliva build up in the air passages and lungs, and can reduce the flow of air and oxygen into the greyhound's respiratory system. This significantly reduces its performance.

Greyhounds that often need biling out will commonly eat grass in a self-induced attempt to clear their system; a frothy grass substance is usually brought up. By vomiting the dog out the bile will be brought up from the intestine, and this process is thought to help clear the lungs and air passages as well.

While most trainers tend to bile a dog out several days before a race, I personally have found it quite beneficial to bile out on the morning of a race; in my experience a lot of dogs perform exceptionally well when vomited out in this way. Indeed, if I were going to place a nice bet on one of my dogs, I would often bile them out on the morning of the race.

To bile out, give the dog a bowl of warm milk, an egg and a knob of butter mixed up. After about five minutes put three or four soda crystals down the dog's throat to try and induce it to vomit. The dog should then be left for a couple of hours to rest in its kennel before it is given any food or fluids.

THE SEASONAL CYCLE

When carrying out your grooming routine and general check of the feet and teeth, the bitch should be checked for signs that she is coming on heat, or for any sign of infection. The majority of bitches will break in season every six months, but this is not a hard and fast rule and some bitches will break yearly and others every nine months. A good handler should know his bitches and have a reasonable idea when they are about to break season; it also makes life easier to keep a record of each individual bitch.

The majority of bitches when they are about to break season will run really well – though this is not always the case, and some will go the opposite way and run really badly. It is therefore important that the handler knows the traits of each bitch and how they run before they break season – especially if he likes a bit of a flutter!

When the bitch is about to break you should notice a change in her behaviour: she will become skittish and lively, she will take great delight in raising her tail at any nearby male dog, and then proceed to snap his head off if he comes near. These are sure signs that the bitch is about to break heat.

When a bitch has broken heat she should be isolated from any dogs for at least three weeks to avoid any chance of an unwanted mating. At around five weeks she should start to produce milk, and it is at this point that any serious work should cease until she is back to normal. A splash of cider vinegar in her evening meal can often help disperse any lingering milk.

As the bitch draws out of season she will usually start to come to hand at around the sixteenth or seventeenth week. Again, if the trainer has kept records and knows his dogs, then there is a good chance that he can pull off a little gamble. If possible I like to try and keep my bitches' season dates close to my chest, because you can leave a bitch off from racing for fourteen weeks to seventeen weeks and really get to work on her. In this time a good trainer should be able to pull a few good lengths out of a bitch, which should undoubtedly win a race.

When checking the vagina the handler should be aware of any changes, such as irregular bleeding or discharge. Any such problems will need the skills of a veterinarian, so don't delay in getting the bitch looked at.

Checking the Male Greyhound

When checking the male greyhound the handler should be aware of any yellow-green type discharge from the penis. This condition is known as balanitis, and affected dogs can often be seen with evidence of this discharge down the inside of the leg. The infection can then be transported to the mouth and stomach, and cause other unwanted problems.

Treatment involves cleaning the area with a solution of Dettol and warm water, using a swab of cotton wool. As you clean the area, wipe and then throw away, wipe and throw away, using several swabs of cotton wool in the process. If any secondary infections of the mouth or throat have occurred, or the penis isn't clearing up after a week, then veterinary advice should be sought.

ADMINISTERING MEDICATION

Giving a Pill

For a novice, giving a greyhound a pill or tablet may seem like hard work. Some trainers like to give tablets with food, but I prefer to know that the dog has actually swallowed the pill. Simply place the pill in your right hand and hold the upper jaw or snout with your left hand and lift the dog's head up. With this the mouth should start to open and you can push the pill right to the back of the throat. Close the dog's mouth and rub its throat, and hopefully the pill should be gone. If not, and it is still in the mouth, then you need to use your index finger to push it a little deeper down the throat.

Giving Liquid Medication

It is easiest to give liquid medication with a syringe, and depending on the dosage you can use a different sized syringe. Administer the dose in the same way as a tablet: stand over the dog so that you are in full control of it, hold the top of the snout, and lift it back so that the dog opens its mouth. The liquid can then be administered to the back of the mouth, which should be closed quickly to stop the dog spitting it out. If the liquid tastes vile then the dog may well resist your attempts to administer it, so it is important to try and accomplish the task first time.

CHAPTER EIGHT

The Ailing Greyhound

A general examination can be used to determine if your dog is sick, off colour, or maybe something a little more sinister. By picking up symptoms at an early stage the trainer can get the dog to a veterinarian for a more thorough check and treatment. In cases of serious illness it can be imperative that the dog is seen by a vet at the earliest point – sometimes a delay in getting expert treatment can literally be the difference between life and death.

CONDUCTING AN EXAMINATION

The examination begins with just watching the dog's behaviour; this may well start when you take him out of the kennel:

- Is the dog his usual self?
- Has he been off his food?
- Have his faeces been normal?
- Is the urine discoloured, and is it flowing freely?
- Has the dog been settled, or has he been getting up and down off the bed?
- Did he struggle to get off the bed?
- Has he been showing any signs of discomfort?

After getting the dog out, just observe him for a minute:

- Is he feeling the cold?
- Is the hair on his back standing up, or is he arching his back?

- How is his breathing: is he panting excessively?

Have a look at the dog's eyes:

- Are they bright and healthy, or do they look dull?
- Is there any discharge?
- Do they look sunken? Dogs that are very poorly will sometimes have that sunken eye look, so be aware of this.

Check the dog's ears for any inflammation, discharge or general soreness.

Next, check the dog's mouth:

- Does his breath smell foul?
- Check the gums for any paleness; this can be a good indication of anaemia.
- Is there any swelling or redness around the back of the throat or tonsils?
- While checking the mouth, make sure it is free of any growths.
- Has he been coughing?

Gently stroke down the dog's windpipe to check for any signs of discomfort; if he has kennel cough the inflammation in his windpipe will undoubtedly be irritating and will more than likely cause him to cough. While kennel cough is the most common cause of coughing for the greyhound, there are other problems that cause coughing, some of which can be quite serious.

Check the dog's feet and body for any cuts, sores or bites that may be painful or infected;

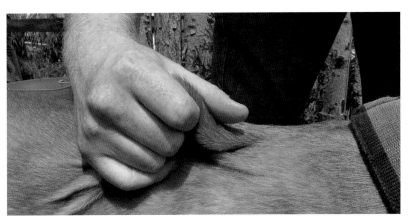

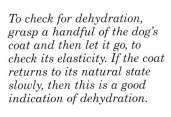

To check for dehydration, grasp a handful of the dog's coat and then let it go, to check its elasticity. If the coat returns to its natural state slowly, then this is a good indication of dehydration.

even minor infections can become quite serious if left unnoticed and untreated.

Check the dog for signs of dehydration by lifting a handful of his skin up on his back, then letting it drop again: in its normal state the skin should return quickly, if the dog is dehydrated then the skin will return much more slowly. Also his coat may well appear dull and dry.

Taking the Temperature

If you are unhappy with the dog's apparent state of health, you may feel that you need to investigate further. A very important piece of equipment is the thermometer to read its temperature, and every trainer should possess at least one.

The thermometer should be shaken a little to settle the mercury, and coated with an antibacterial lubricant. It should then be placed into the rectum and held there for around thirty seconds to get a reading; the length of time needed for this may vary, but should be given with the thermometer. The dog's normal reading should be 38.3°C (101°F) in a state of rest; however, if it has just run a race it may well be slightly elevated. A reading of 38.8–39.4°C (101–102°F) is a good indication of a mild fever; anything more than this should be considered serious, and it would be wise to seek veterinary attention.

If you are a complete novice, any rise in the dog's temperature should prompt you to get a second opinion. While you may not want to appear over-zealous, it is better to be safe than sorry. Also you should never miss the opportunity to learn from somebody more knowledgeable than you.

A sure sign that the dog has a problem is a rise in its temperature; it may be caused by an infection, disease, a cold or flu-like virus, blood poisoning, an abscess, or a reaction to an injury.

Much worse than the high temperature is the sub-normal temperature: a dog with a temperature of below 37.7°C (100°F) is not at all well, and should be taken to a veterinarian immediately.

Taking the Pulse

After checking the dog's temperature, take the pulse: do this by checking the large femoral artery which lies underneath the hind leg, just in front of the groin. If you place one of your index fingers on the artery where it is located on the femur bone you should be able to feel the dog's heartbeat pulse; this should be around seventy beats a minute when the dog is at rest, and the rhythm should be four or five beats and then a missed beat – this is quite normal.

A fast beat, a slow beat, or a dog that has infrequent missed beats are all good indications of a problem, although a slow beat is likely to be more of a problem than a fast one.

For the novice it would be good practice to periodically check a healthy dog's temperature and pulse so that he can get a good indication of what they should be in their healthy state. If the

First Aid

As a trainer or handler you may find that from time to time you have to deal with a situation that requires veterinary assistance. Due to the nature of the greyhound and the way he is trained, he is susceptible to any sort of injury: for example a dog may fall in the paddock and break its leg, or it may run into a fence and cut itself wide open while coursing. At these times the trainer will need to address the emergency and patch the dog up until it can be presented to a veterinarian. For this reason it is quite imperative that the novice handler has some sort of basic first aid skills.

A good trainer will always have a good first aid kit; you can't have enough kit, so always make sure you're well stocked up.

Basic First Aid Kit
Surgical scissors
Tweezers
Splints
Cotton wool
Cotton bandage
Self-adhesive bandage
Dettol
TCP
Kaolin poultice
Animalintex (poultice)
Antiseptic wound powder
Hydrogen peroxide
Needle and surgical thread
Penicillin tube
Penicillin injection
Most trainers usually have access to painkillers and antibiotics.

Open Wounds
If the dog has an open wound then it is important to try and stop or reduce the bleeding. This can be done by soaking some cotton wool in a solution of Dettol and water, and then placing it with a firm pressure on the wound. This should help clean and disinfect the wound while stopping the bleeding. Depending on its location, a firm bandage may be applied until the wound can be examined by a veterinarian.

If the wound is not too bad, then an experienced handler may well clean it and put in a couple of stitches himself if needed; this is an emergency resort, however, and it is always best to call a vet, particularly as a course of antibiotics will almost certainly be required.

Splinting a Broken Leg
A dog that has sustained a lower leg fracture may need a temporary splint putting on until it can be attended by a veterinarian. It is important that the splint is positioned so that it covers the injured bone above and below the upper and lower joint of the injured limb. The dog may well become distressed, so it is important to try and keep him calm and in a quiet environment; simply patting and talking to him can be of great reassurance. If you can get in touch with the vet

novice waits until a dog is ill before he ever tries to take any readings then he may struggle to tell any difference, unless there was a big change.

It is a good idea to keep a close eye on a dog's stools. Any dog passing diarrhoea should be watched carefully, and diarrhoea should never be taken lightly. I have known dogs contract gastroenteritis and be dead within twenty-four hours. If you are a novice, don't leave it a couple of days to see if clears up: be on the safe side and get the dog checked by a vet.

As well as diarrhoea, keep an eye out for vomiting; greyhounds are often sick in their bed and hide the evidence underneath the bedding.

If you are an accomplished trainer you may well be happy with your own diagnosis, and may not feel that you need to get further advice. However, if you are a novice, or in any case where there is doubt as to what is wrong, the veterinarian is only a phone call away, so don't be afraid to call him.

MINOR AILMENTS

There are so many minor illnesses or complaints that it would be impossible as a trainer to have experienced them all. Some of these problems will need veterinary assistance, so it is important that as a trainer you can recognize the ones you encounter.

For ease of reference for the reader, the problems that are dealt with here are arranged in alphabetical order.

you can hopefully get some advice on administering painkillers to him.

Applying a Bandage

It is important that a novice handler knows how to put on a bandage correctly. The usual area for the greyhound to be bandaged is around the lower limbs, such as the wrist, the hock or the toes.

When applying a bandage, cotton wool should first be placed between each of the toes to protect them. It is important that the toes are bandaged; if they are left free, then they can severely swell up. Cotton wool or a cotton wool-type bandage can then be placed around the limb, followed by a self-adhesive bandage such as vetwrap; soak the cotton wool or material in the Dettol solution before applying it to an open wound.

The bandage should only be put on tightly if you are putting a pressure bandage on a wound to try and stop the flow of bleeding. If you put a bandage on tightly and leave it on, then the circulation to the limb will be reduced, and if you leave a bandage on like this for any length of time, you may create some serious problems. I saw a dog many years ago that had been bandaged too tightly, and when the bandage was removed after a few days its leg had become gangrenous and it ended up losing it.

Applying a Poultice

Apply a kaolin poultice as follows: first, heat up the tub of poultice until it is hot. Test the kaolin with your elbow to make sure it is not too hot, and then apply it to a strip of cotton wool or square bandage. It can then be applied to the problem area and a bandage applied. Kaolin poultice is commonly used for drawing foreign objects or pus from wounds; however, it can be used on thickened joints. A good example of this is a dog with an old and on-going wrist problem such as arthritis. The injury needs to be managed, and the use of cold water therapy and kaolin poultices can have a beneficial effect.

Firstly, hose the wrist off with cold water three or four times a day for forty-eight hours after a race, and then apply a kaolin poultice to the wrist every eight hours until the greyhound is due to race again. I would also combine this with flexion and extension exercises between poultices to try and help stabilize the wrist. With continuous treatment a problem injury can sometimes be managed to keep the dog fit for racing.

The Animalintex poultice – a soft, thick, cotton wool-type material – can be used for similar tasks as the kaolin poultice. Animalintex can be used hot to apply heat to an injury, or it can be soaked in cold water and used to reduce swelling. First soak the poultice in hot or cold water, then squeeze it out and apply it to the problem area. Cotton wool should then be wrapped around it, and a bandage applied.

Animalintex can be used on a multitude of injuries such as tendon or ligament strains or sprains. It can be used for drawing infection or softening corns and warts.

Acidosis

Acidosis is clinically known as exertional rhabdomyolysis, but it is also referred to under several other names, such as 'the screws' and 'running the back of a dog'. Acidosis is seen on different levels, ranging from a mild soreness in the back at one end of the scale, to your dog being a fatality at the other. It can therefore be a very serious condition and should not be taken lightly by the handler.

While acidosis is a problem that is usually seen in the coursing greyhound, it is a problem that can still affect the track-racing dog.

The usual signs are that the dog is very sore across its back; this soreness may well spread into the neck and limbs, depending on the severity of the problem. The dog is likely to find any touch or pressure placed on its back to be very painful. This soreness may well confuse the novice handler, as he may think that his dog has damaged its back muscles or spine.

The dog's pain and distress may be quite severe, and it may have trouble getting on and off its bed; it may drag its feet as it walks because it finds just moving around to be very uncomfortable. Depending how severely it is affected you may also notice that the urine is discoloured or even that there is blood in it. A dog can lose a serious amount of weight in the first week of acidosis. Furthermore it may be forty-eight hours or so before the symptoms of this condition appear.

To appreciate how this condition occurs you need to understand how the body works.

When the body is subject to violent exercise, glycogen is used in the production of energy, but large amounts of the waste product lactic acid are left within the muscles. There are buffers within the muscle cells that neutralize the build-up of this lactic acid, but the problems start when the buffers within the muscles cannot cope with the large workload that is placed upon them. The muscle cells become swollen and muscle waste is leaked into the bloodstream, all of which causes the dog pain and distress.

There are three main situations when acidosis is likely to occur. First, in dogs that are out of condition or have had a long lay-off, and which are then subjected to a workload they cannot cope with. This may also include dogs that are physically fit, but which are then worked beyond their capability to recover, for example a dog that has run an extra lap or two after a race, or a coursing dog that has had an exceptionally long course or courses.

The second situation is when the weather conditions are hot and humid, and a dog gets excited or stressed before racing. This is because when a dog becomes stressed and pants excessively, large amounts of the critical buffer agents are used up before the race, thus leaving the dog in short supply when eventually it runs.

Thirdly, dogs that are overworked with excessive running and trialling could be affected. A very stressful racing programme can affect the chemical balance within the dog's body, and this can bring on a mild form of acidosis.

The handler should waste no time in getting veterinary attention to the affected dog. While acidosis is rarely fatal, it must still be realized that this is a serious problem and a greyhound *could* die within forty-eight hours if it is not given the right treatment. Furthermore acidosis can cause serious weight loss, which a dog can often take a long time to recover from; indeed some dogs never fully recover, and often struggle to regain anything like their best race form.

Prevention is always far better than cure, and the handler can achieve this to a certain degree by making sure the dog is fit enough for the task at hand, and that it has a sound nutritional diet. Vitamin E plays an important role in how efficiently the muscles utilize the oxygen within the muscles; this is useful in that shortage of oxygen within the performing muscles can indirectly increase the likelihood of acidosis. The use of creatine can also be of benefit as it helps in combating the onset of lactic acid. A mild kidney tonic such as Neutradex can also be used when a greyhound is in hard work, to help flush the natural build-up of muscle waste from the system.

Anaemia

The blood is split into two groups, red blood cells and white blood cells. The red cells are used to transport oxygen around the body and also to get rid of the waste products in the blood; the white cells are part of the body's immune system, which staves off any unwanted intruder.

Within the red blood cells there is a protein known as haemoglobin, whose job is to carry the oxygen around the body. When there is a deficiency of haemoglobin within the red blood cells, or when there is any significant decrease in red blood cells, the dog will suffer from anaemia.

A greyhound with anaemia will probably be performing well below his best, and will often take a lot more time to recover after a run. It will appear to be off colour, but without suffering from any identifiable illness. A good indication of a dog that is anaemic is the colour of its gums; they will be much paler than usual. How bad the condition is will depend on how deficient the blood is of red blood cells.

The usual course of action is to increase essential amino acids, iron and vitamin B12 in the diet; however, it is important that the dog is given a full blood test to reveal the true extent of the problem. The vet can then advise the best course of treatment.

Anal Glands

If a dog is observed dragging his backside and licking its rear end it should not be assumed that worm infestation is the problem: it may be that the anal glands need emptying. These glands are situated at the top of the tail and lie on either side of the anus, and can become blocked through an accumulation of waste material. To bring the dog relief they need to be emptied.

Emptying these glands is not necessarily a veterinary procedure, however it is essential that those who have never done this before are shown how to do so either by a vet or an experienced handler.

If the anal glands are left unattended then the risk of infection or further problems is increased. It is worth noting that dogs that have had their glands cleaned will often perform much better the next time they race.

Cuts and Bites

Cuts, bites or any sort of open wound are frequently incurred by the greyhound. If the problem is not too serious then the trainer can often deal with the wound himself.

The hair around the wound should be clipped short, and the wound should be cleaned thoroughly with a solution of warm water and Dettol or TCP. A penicillin stick or antiseptic cream or powder can then be applied to help treat the wound.

If the wound is left matted with dirty hair, bacteria will inevitably get into the wound, and if they get into the bloodstream then infection or even blood poisoning is a likely consequence.

The more experienced trainer will probably be able to put a couple of stitches in a small wound; however, for anything more serious, or if the handler feels he does not have the experience or capability to do a good job, the vet should be called.

When examining any damage it is a good idea to check under the broken skin for any internal damage. Any damage to the underlying muscle, tendon or ligament should be inspected and treated by a veterinarian.

Dehydration

Dehydration can be a common problem for the greyhound, but it is a problem that can easily be missed, especially by the novice. The dog's coat may well look dull and listless, the skin will lose its elasticity and will return to its normal state very slowly when pulled up, and the dog may well run off or lose weight.

There are two main causes of dehydration. First, a dog that is not provided with a readily available supply of water and electrolyte replacement may well suffer from dehydration. This is easily remedied by supplying the dog with the necessary water. Some trainers believe that it is not necessary to provide the dog with water in the kennel, and maintain that it gets enough liquid through its food – that is, the milk and gravy supplied in the meals. My personal conviction is that every dog should have water available to it twenty-four hours a day; a lot can be learned about a dog's state of health by how much water it has drunk.

Dogs that pant a lot in hot weather, that bark excessively, that are excitable, and dogs that are fed a lot of dried food will have a tendency to become dehydrated.

Secondly, the dog can become dehydrated through illness or disease; excessive vomiting or diarrhoea can certainly be a problem.

If a dog has a readily available supply of water and you feel that it is dehydrated nonetheless, then it is advisable to call a vet to examine it.

Diarrhoea

Diarrhoea in the greyhound should always be taken seriously, especially when there is blood evident. Indeed, with a serious case of gastroenteritis the outcome can sometimes be fatal. There are two types of diarrhoea, acute and chronic: acute diarrhoea is of sudden onset and can last for a few days; chronic diarrhoea is a more sustained condition, where the dog suffers frequently occurring problems with its faeces.

Causes of Acute Diarrhoea
- A change of diet, or a change of kennel, which is a likely cause of a diet change.
- Anything that's off, especially meat that has turned a bit sour.

- Picking up anything that's dead and eating it while taking exercise.
- An allergic reaction to a food substance such as milk; when the substance is removed, the diarrhoea usually subsides.
- Bacterial infections such as salmonella, picked up through eating rancid meat, or as a result of unhygienic conditions where food is prepared.
- Overfeeding a dog when trying to build him up; instead of giving him one large dinner, try giving him three or four lighter meals in the course of the day.
- Enteritis is a frequent problem in the greyhound, causing inflammation of the bowels.
- Canine parvovirus, where diarrhoea is a major symptom.

Greyhounds with acute diarrhoea should ideally be seen by a vet to rule out anything nasty. The dog should be taken off food for a mini-mum of twenty-four hours; when food is reintroduced it should be given in small amounts and should be something easy on the stomach, such as rice.

If there is a lot of blood in the faeces and the dog is vomiting it is important to get immediate veterinary assistance. I have seen greyhounds die within twenty-four hours of passing blood, so not doing anything to see what happens may prove costly.

Causes of Chronic Diarrhoea
Chronic diarrhoea is a continuing problem often caused by worms, dietary factors or an ongoing bowel problem. Veterinary advice should be taken to get to the root of the trouble.

Kennel Cough

Kennel cough is usually a bacterial infection that causes irritation of the windpipe and the connective pipes to the lungs. These pipes may

The thumb and forefinger can be used with a light pressure to feel the windpipe. By gently stroking down the pipe, any soreness or irritation will usually cause the dog to cough.

well become inflamed and sore, which will inevitably cause the dog to cough.

Gentle pressure along the length of the wind-pipe with finger and thumb will usually cause the dog to cough when you press the infection. By this simple test you can often determine if the problem is plain kennel cough or a more sinister lung infection. It is also advisable to take the dog's temperature, as it is likely to be mildly elevated.

The affected greyhound should be quarantined to try and suppress the spread of the problem, and veterinary advice should be taken, or the infected dog or dogs should be taken for examination.

It is important that the handler washes his/her hands when the infected dog has been handled, its feed bowls should be washed with anti-bacterial washing-up liquid, and a paddock should be washed down between the different dogs that use it. As many precautions as possible should be taken to try and contain the spread of kennel cough, as it is highly contagious.

Muscle Cramp

Muscle cramp is a sudden spasm of the muscles in the back, the hindquarters or the forelimb. It is seen more often in the hind limbs or specifically the gracalis, as these are the muscles that cope with a large portion of the work. Indeed the affected limbs may contract to the point that the muscle becomes almost paralysed and the dog may collapse because it cannot stand on its own feet. This sort of severe cramp is likely to be very painful, and it is not unusual for dogs to cry out or yelp when it occurs.

Racing cramp is not always this severe, however, and quite often the symptoms will only be noticed when the dog is gathered up at the end of a race or trial; by the time it has walked back to the racing kennels all signs of cramp will have disappeared. Directly after the race you may find that the cramp can sometimes last a few minutes; massaging, stretching and trying to get the dog moving should help relieve it.

The onset of cramp is well documented, and it is thought that there are several contributing factors that could well be the cause behind any bout of cramp. While the onset of cramp can happen at any time, there are some dogs that are prone to cramp on a cold night and when the temperature drops sharply.

Generally, however, there are two main problems behind racing cramp: nutrition and exercise. Furthermore it is often out-of-condition dogs that suffer from cramp.

When the greyhound runs, its body undergoes certain chemical reactions within the muscles. However, if its body is not conditioned to the point where it can cope with these chemical reactions, it becomes a problem, because when it cannot get rid of the muscle waste products sufficiently, the muscles become less efficient, which can often be seen as the onset of cramp.

It is important that the trainer raises the dog's level of fitness so that it transports oxygen and glycogen into the muscles and then takes all the waste products out. By doing this more efficiently the onset of fatigue and muscle cramp can be delayed until the dog can cope with the full workload.

The step up in workload should be done gradually; thus walking and jogging with the dog can be stepped up in distance in stages, and short sharp gallops accompanied with a good massage can be incorporated to build up fitness.

Secondly, it is important that the dog has a sound nutritional programme. If the greyhound's body is not supplied with the correct vitamins and minerals, then it cannot function efficiently. I would put the dog on a multi-vitamin such as Feramo greyhound or SA-37, and I would also supplement with vitamin E and a mild kidney tonic such as Neutradex.

However, there can be different problems that are causing the dog to cramp, so it is good advice to have your dog checked by a veterinary surgeon. Often urine and blood samples can pinpoint the problem, and the dog can be treated with medication. The vet will then be able to prescribe a more detailed or tailored therapy for your dog.

The Salivary Duct

Damage to the salivary duct will appear as a swelling underneath the dog's jaw and around the top of the neck. The swelling can be quite severe and is often caused through a knock or bang to its face.

While the problem seems to cause the dog no physical pain or stress, it must be rather uncomfortable for it to have to run with it. To repair the problem the dog will have to have surgery. In most cases when the fluid is only drained off, then the problem resurfaces shortly afterwards.

Skin Problems

The dog's skin and hair play an important role in its wellbeing. The skin not only acts as a protective barrier against the outside world, it also helps the dog perceive its environment through the nerve endings within the skin.

Mange

Mange is a mite infestation and can be a real problem for the greyhound trainer; the dog will often chew and scratch itself in a bid to relieve the itchiness. The most common area of mange is down the bottom of the hind legs and on the belly and chest. There is usually a loss of hair, and the skin will appear red and sore; it is usually accompanied by a fusty smell.

While some dogs experience only mild soreness and hair loss, I have seen the occasional dog with 50 to 60 per cent of its body affected. These cases can be very difficult to put right even with extensive veterinary care.

In mild cases shampoos and creams will often cure the problem, but if the mange persists the vet may well have to take a skin scraping to get a more detailed look at the problem. Yellow sulphur or sulphur tablets can be used to cool the blood; this is an old-fashioned method which helps treat the problem from the inside out. I have also had some success with a charcoal and tar shampoo obtainable from most pet shops; I found this more successful than most expensive medicated shampoos. When bathing a dog with mange always wear protective gloves; the disposable sort are usually the best.

Mange can be highly contagious, so it is important that affected dogs are kept in quarantine to stop the spread of the problem.

Chilblains

Cracks and splits that appear on the tip of the dog's ear or ears are known as chilblains. The split ear will usually bleed a lot and can often take some stopping. The dog will often shake its head relentlessly or scratch its head until the ear starts bleeding again.

The use of antibiotic cream or wound powder can be effective, and a stocking or scarf can be placed over the head to protect the ears from scratching or head shaking. If the ears are in a bad state or are not healing then I would suggest you take veterinary advice.

Capped Elbow

Capped elbow is usually caused when a dog has been sleeping on a hard surface; this could be due to a lack of bedding or from the dog just sleeping on the floor. The elbow will fill with fluid, and can become quite large if left unattended. In its initial stage it may well be sore, swollen and painful, so the application of an ice pack can be beneficial for the first seven to ten days. In cases of extreme swelling the elbow can be drained off and an anti-inflammatory cream could be used.

Split Tail

A split tail can be a real nightmare for the handler; the dog seems to take great pleasure in giving you a nice red spray job every time you get him out of the kennel.

The damage is usually caused by a dog repeatedly shaking himself and whipping his tail against the wall or bed.

If the tail is only cracked at its end then you may be able to treat it without surgery. The old-fashioned way is to stop the bleeding with some hydrogen peroxide, and then place the tip of the tail in a small tub of friar's balsam. The tail will then need padding with cotton wool and strapping up as best as possible.

Dogs with serious injury to the tail end will no doubt need surgery; the end one or two caudal vertebrae may need to be amputated if the tail is to heal properly.

A badly damaged tail end, usually the result of the dog flicking it against the kennel wall or door.

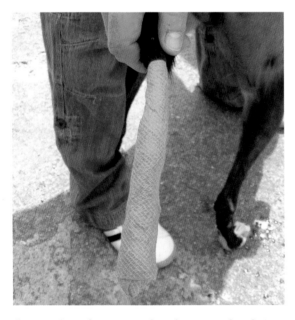

A strapping of cotton wool and vetwrap has been placed on the tail to help protect it and to prevent further damage. This bandage should be changed daily, and the tail examined; if there is any doubt as to the progress of healing, the dog should be taken to a veterinarian for a check.

Tonsillitis

The tonsils are situated at the back of the throat and their purpose is to regulate any infection coming in through the mouth. Tonsillitis is caused either by a throat infection, or by the dog licking at an infected wound. Symptoms may include enlarged tonsils, difficulty eating, a rise in temperature, and excessive salivation (froth around the lips and mouth).

When checking for tonsillitis you need to look for any inflammation or redness of the tonsils. Open the mouth wide and use your index finger to hold down the tongue to get a clear view of them. You also need to check the dog for any obvious signs of infection, where it may have been licking; this could be a cut or a wound that has become infected, or an infection to the penis, the vagina or the anus.

What treatment is given depends on the severity of the tonsillitis and how it affects the dog. In severe cases the dog may well lose race performance and general condition; it may also have an accompanying dry cough. It is important that the dog is checked by a veterinarian, as a course of antibiotics is probably the best option for treatment. Removal of the tonsils may also be considered; however, there are cases where greyhounds lose significant race form after this operation, and this loss of form is sometimes permanent, the dog struggling to regain its best performances.

Track Leg

The track leg is a swelling on the inside of the tibia, and is the indirect result of the foreleg striking the tibia on passage. Underlying injury will cause the greyhound to run with an unorthodox action, so that the foreleg (between the elbow and the wrist) strikes the tibia (shin) as it passes.

The track leg can be seen in various forms, from a minor swelling on the bone to a large, solid thickening of the bone, the result of an old progressed injury. The actual swelling is the result of bruising and bleeding of the surface layer of the bone and the local blood vessels. A hard, lumpy thickening to the bone is an indication of a well progressed injury,

Track leg. Notice the swelling to the nearside leg.

where the bone has become scarred and damaged, and a long-standing problem.

The track leg is a secondary injury and is caused by an abnormal gait, which is generally thought of as being the result of a shoulder or a hip injury.

When detecting a track leg in its minor stage – or indeed at any stage where there is any accompanying swelling, however minor – it must be considered that the primary injury is still active. By this I would suggest that the injury causing the problem is still causing the dog some grief, so it is important to pinpoint and correct the primary injury or injuries.

It is commonly thought that track leg is generally caused by a shoulder injury. But even if this is the case, it must also be considered that the shoulder injury is a secondary injury itself, and a deeper problem is more than likely the culprit behind both of these injuries.

In my experience I have found that many dogs that have a track leg will also have a lower neck problem; this may well be seen in the cervical-thoracic (c-t) junction or around the musculature of the lower neck. It is important that these injuries are dealt with if the track leg is going to remain injury free. All this aside, I would recommend that a thorough investigation is undertaken to establish any further problems.

To see if there is any contact while the dog is running, place a very thin layer of petroleum jelly on the track leg; after the run, check the outside of the foreleg to see if there has been any contact. High contact is often associated with front-end damage, while a lower contact is often considered to be a hind-limb problem.

Even after the track leg has been treated and the mitigating injury has been corrected, it can still be a good idea to put Vaseline on the tibia to check for any further contact.

PROBLEMS OF TEMPERAMENT

Excitable Dogs

A greyhound that is very excitable can cause the handler a few problems; these dogs often bounce off the walls in the kennel, go loopy when let off the lead, and tend to run their race in the kennel before they even make it on to the track. They are often prone to cramp, and can 'train off' or struggle to keep any sort of race form.

Introducing vitamin E into the diet can help the dog settle down and run with a little more consistency; there are several supplements on the market.

The excitable dog can often become dehydrated, so it is important to keep an eye on its intake of water.

Some dogs are prone to jumping around the kennel, and to pre-empt this behaviour a low 'ceiling' could be constructed. Using a material such as chipboard or strong wire mesh, a temporary ceiling could be put in the kennel at about 1.25m (4ft); this would stop the dog constantly jumping up and down.

Fighters

A greyhound that fights or turns its head during a race can be a real nightmare for the owner or trainer. These dogs are usually disqualified from racing if they fight on more than one occasion; at some tracks, however, they will not race a dog if it has fought or had its card marked. There are several reasons a dog might fight:

- Young puppies or playful dogs often chase the other dogs rather than the hare; these dogs are usually quite daft, but don't have a bad bone in their body.
- Some greyhounds don't chase the hare 100 per cent and often lose concentration; some are schooled on a certain type of hare, and sometimes will only chase that one type.
- The use of anabolic therapy can cause the greyhound to become more aggressive, which can relate to its behaviour on the track.
- Some trainers feel the need to give their dogs live prey to make them keen, but this practice can sometimes push a dog 'over the edge' and cause it to fight.
- A greyhound that is carrying an injury and is sore may well have a tendency to 'turn its head'. In this case it should always be given a thorough check over in case it has gone lame or is carrying an injury.

While some greyhounds are blatant fighters, others are maybe just little understood. Certainly, not every dog should be 'tarred with the same brush', as it must be considered that there are several types of fighter:

- Some greyhounds will fight at any available opportunity. These are usually young dogs that soon get disqualified, and there is little hope of straightening them out.
- Some greyhounds will turn their head or occasionally actually fight, but if it's not blatant fighting, it's not always picked up. These dogs will usually run much better fresh and it is important not to run them too often, especially on the same track.
- Some greyhounds will have a little look or a glance across at another dog now and again. Depending on the racing manager and the dog in question, the incident may well be overlooked. If the dog hasn't shown any previous problems, I would suggest you give it a rest.
- Lastly there is the dodger who just waits in front but never actually turns his head or shows any aggression to any other dog. These dogs often like to be in the photo finish picture, but will usually take great pleasure in getting beaten a short head if you have a flutter on them. They will often wait in front until another dog comes past them, when they will quicken up and run with the lead dog.

There are several options for the handler:

- Racing a dog over hurdles can sometimes be an option for the dog that likes a little nibble during a race. It will have to concentrate a lot harder, which gives it less opportunity to fight. However, it should be noted that every dog that runs over hurdles is not a fighter.
- A greyhound can be kept fresh and alert by changing tracks; it could also be given unofficial trials at other tracks to try and keep it straight.
- Some dogs don't chase certain types of lure: there are inside hares, outside hares, Sumner hares and McGee hares, and I have seen some dogs fight on one type of hare but on another they will chase 100 per cent.

It can be very frustrating for the handler, especially if the greyhound is very, very fast. In the early 1990s I was involved with an incredibly fast animal that contested several major finals. This dog very rarely won a race but ran second to many of the fastest dogs on the circuit; the dog would never turn his head, but managed to get beaten by a short head a lot of times.

Kennel Fights

In a large kennel environment it is inevitable that at some point a fight will break out between two or more dogs. When more than two dogs are involved it is usually one unfortunate dog in particular that gets set upon. Even if the dogs are muzzled it can be quite a task to get the situation under control.

If the dogs are not muzzled it is unwise to try and separate them with your hands; find whatever comes to hand, such as a brush or shovel, to try and get between the dogs and separate them. If possible throw a bucket of water on them in an attempt to startle them.

Injuries from fights can be anything from bites and tears to the skin and musculature, to stiffness and bruising. It is important that the handler closely examines all the dogs involved so he can get to grips with any problems.

Nervousness

Nervous greyhounds are not uncommon; these dogs are often shy or timid in the presence of an unknown person or object, and in many cases it is a man the dog feels uncomfortable with. There are varying levels of nervousness: some dogs will just be frightened and cower down, while others will be terrified and will desperately try to escape the situation.

It is often suggested that a nervous dog has been beaten or ill treated to act in the manner it does. While in some cases this may be true, I would suggest it is not always the case. I have seen pups that have been reared from birth in the same fashion as their siblings, but for some reason one of the litter is very nervy and uneasy around people.

The nervous dog usually takes well to one person, but it is important that other people or kennel workers try to form a bond with it. The dog could be given extra attention and some one-on-one care every day to try and calm its nerves. If you let a nervous dog off the lead in a paddock at home, it is a good idea to leave a collar on, with a short bit of rope or lead attached; this will give you something to get hold of if the dog proves difficult to catch – though it should not be so long that it trips him up as he walks or trots about.

When you take a dog like this into your kennel it is advisable to let it settle in and form a bond before taking it to the race track. This type of dog is often very difficult to catch at the hare trip, and you may find you can't catch it at all. It is important not to get frustrated and shout at it, however, as this will only cause it to panic and make it even more difficult to catch.

When trying to catch the dog you should walk away from it, or rattle a sweet bag to try and coax it to come to you. Never chase or run after it as it will always run away from you. Another option is to walk back to the kennel area and try and coax the dog to follow you; if this fails another handler could bring a familiar dog on to the track to try and lure the dog to you.

The nervous dog is often a picky eater, and when it comes into a new environment the handler may well have trouble getting it to eat. If it keeps turning up its nose at its food it is a good idea to feed it something tasty. Pilchards mixed up with rice pudding is a good concoction to persuade a nervy dog to eat, then day by day a little more of your daily food can be added to switch it on to a normal diet.

With a nervous dog it is important to remember that a lot of patience is needed.

Thin Greyhounds

Some greyhounds are very light framed and it is a struggle to make them gain weight; to add to the problem they are often picky eaters. When a dog is in constant training, trying to get any weight on it can be particularly difficult. Feeding it lighter meals but on a much more frequent basis can be beneficial. At breakfast time, honey can be used on the feed to try and encourage it to eat. Adding a spoonful of sunflower oil once a day can also add some extra calories while trying to build the dog up, though I wouldn't suggest giving this on a long-term basis as it contains toxins and can raise cholesterol.

If the dog is a really bad eater, putting oily fish such as sardines on the meal will usually get the dog's taste buds going and help it to eat its meal. I have never yet known a dog turn up its nose at fish.

If the dog is not on a vitamin supplement then I would suggest that this can also be of great benefit.

Greyhounds that are thin and struggle to put weight on are sometimes stressful animals. A dog that stands and barks all day should be moved to a quieter kennel if possible. One that gets worked up at feed time should be fed first, to avoid this problem. By making some simple changes you can sometimes solve a lot of problems.

SERIOUS CONDITIONS

There are many serious conditions that affect the greyhound – or indeed any dog. These conditions will almost certainly require veterinary assistance, but as a trainer it is important that you recognize some of the symptoms; outlined below are a few of the more serious conditions that might be encountered.

Canine Distemper

Canine distemper is a serious viral disease that can be fatal, is incurable, and is very contagious between dogs; however, it cannot be passed on to humans. The infection is more commonly associated with young puppies, especially those between three to six months. The disease is spread through bodily fluids such as urine and faeces, so it is important that any infected animal is quarantined immediately.

The first signs of the illness are a runny nose, a slight discharge in the eyes and a fever. Following this there will be gastric problems such as diarrhoea, vomiting and dehydration. In severe cases the central nervous system may be attacked, causing involuntary muscle twitching or even seizures; however, these symptoms may not develop straightaway.

The best way to prevent canine distemper is to inoculate your dogs. This is an annual inoculation, and it is a strict ruling of the NGRC that if a dog has no inoculation certificate it cannot trial or race.

Canine Influenza

Canine influenza or dog flu is a virus that can cause joint pain, fever and respiratory problems. There are two forms of influenza, one more serious than the other. In the mild form the dog will develop a soft, moist cough and a nasal discharge that could last for up to a month; these symptoms could easily be mistaken for kennel cough. In more severe cases the dog may have an accompanying fever and signs of pneumonia. It is thought that a large number of dogs actually contract the disease but rarely show any of the symptoms. The majority of dogs that do show symptoms will show only mild signs of the disease, and only a small number ever develops a serious condition. The fatality rate is low.

Epilepsy

Epilepsy, or fits, is quite a rare condition in the greyhound, but occasionally a dog is affected. The fits can happen at any time of the day or night. As in the human condition, the dog will collapse to the ground and its legs will peddle back and forth at a frantic pace. The teeth will chatter and snap, so it is advisable to place an object such as a stick between the teeth to prevent the dog biting its own tongue. During the fit the dog will be unconscious, and will have no awareness of anything going on around him.

There is not much the handler can do to prevent an epilectic fit, because its onset will be entirely unexpected. While the dog is having a fit a cold wet towel can be placed over it, and any objects that could do the dog harm should be moved. It is likely that the fit may last several minutes, and the other dogs in the kennel get upset and excited because they don't understand what's happening. If the dog has a kennel mate it is important to remove it from the kennel, because in its excited state it could well bite or attack the epileptic dog.

Enteritis

There are various forms of enteritis, the most common being gastroenteritis. The main symptoms are depression, reluctance to eat, slight fever, vomiting and diarrhoea. The diarrhoea will often start watery, but will turn dark brown in colour and may progress to a red blood colour; it will have a distinct smell that you can detect as soon as you set foot in your kennels.

The condition will usually spread to several dogs in your kennel so it is important to try and quarantine any infected dogs. In severe cases it can be fatal, and a dog can die within twenty-four hours of its first symptoms, so it is important that veterinary assistance or advice is sought as soon as possible.

Packed Cell Volume

The opposite of anaemia is a serious but relatively rare condition called 'packed cell volume'. Its distinctive feature is a rise in the number of red blood cells, with the result that the blood becomes so thick that the heart struggles to pump it round the body. The ensuing problem is that oxygen is then not delivered to the body tissue at a rate sufficient to satisfy the needs of the body when the dog is put under any immense physical stress. The result is that when the dog runs a race, oxygen cannot be pumped to the muscles and brain fast enough, so that after the race the dog may struggle to breathe and may even collapse. A dog I had that suffered from this condition never recovered from it, even after extensive veterinary investigation.

Over the years there have been a few occasions where I have seen a dog collapse and die at the trip, even after performing well; PCV could therefore be an explanation for an apparently healthy dog dropping dead after a race.

Parvovirus

Canine parvovirus appeared in the late 1970s and is similar to feline panleukopenia in cats. The disease affects animals such as dogs, wolves and foxes, but is not contagious to birds or humans, although it is possible for birds to carry the disease or spread the virus by pecking at infected faeces.

The disease is highly contagious and can quickly spread through a number of dogs in a kennel environment. However, a large percentage of infected dogs will not show any of the symptoms of parvovirus in the early stages of the condition.

Within three to ten days of the dog developing the disease it may start showing symptoms such as vomiting, diarrhoea and fever. It is not unusual for the diarrhoea to be very watery or to contain a lot of blood; in severe cases a greyhound can die within twenty-four hours, so it is essential that any dog showing these symptoms is given immediate veterinary attention.

It is very important that all dogs are inoculated against parvovirus because not only is it very contagious, it is also extremely resilient: it can survive in extreme weather conditions, and can only be destroyed with bleach.

Due to the nature of parvovirus it is important that all infected dogs are quarantined, and that any faeces are cleaned up promptly and the area thoroughly disinfected.

Pneumonia

Pneumonia is an inflammation of the lung, and is often the result of an infection, or a physical injury. The symptoms include coughing, chest pain, fever and difficulty breathing, which could easily be mistaken for ordinary kennel cough. However, unlike kennel cough, the cough will be much deeper and huskier, and the dog may become dehydrated and reluctant to eat.

It is important that the dog is given immediate veterinary attention because pneumonia can be fatal. It will also need extensive, high quality nursing if it is to make a good recovery. It is essential that it is kept in a warm, dry kennel with plenty of quiet so that it can rest undisturbed.

NOTE: Whenever you handle a sick dog it is important always to wash your hands with an anti-bacterial soap before you touch any other dog, food or utensils.

CHAPTER NINE

The Injuries Incurred by the Racing Greyhound

THE CAUSES OF INJURIES

Injuries to the racing or coursing greyhound are very complex, the muscles, tendons, ligaments and bones making up a complicated piece of machinery that propels the greyhound at high speed. It must be appreciated that due to the stresses that are placed upon the greyhound's structure, injuries of some description are inevitable each time the greyhound puts its paws upon the race track. For this reason the day-to-day examination should be seen as a critical part of any trainer's daily routine. It is important that the trainer becomes familiar with some of the most common injury sites and also how they can be detected. It must also be noted that when any injury is established by the handler, veterinary advice must be sought so that the correct treatment can be administered or advised.

The greyhound is a very fast animal capable of accelerating from a standing start to top speed in an extremely short space of time. It is also unique in that, unlike in any other sport, it has to perform at maximum output with little or no opportunity to warm up. The short time available from the kennel being opened to the greyhound going into the traps is

Noirs Ted (Trap 6, left of shot) getting turned sideways at the first bend, Peterborough Stadium, 13 May 2008. (© Steve Nash Photography)

nowhere near sufficient for it to have had any serious warming-up time. This lack of pre-race warm-up will inevitably leave the greyhound's physical structure unprepared for the task at hand, and this alone will increase the risk of damage and/or trauma.

The racing greyhound is expected to negotiate an oval circuit with bends that can be perilously tight – and not only this, but the distance to the first bend is often too long, which means the dog will be travelling at top speed when it hits the first corner. It must also be considered that the greyhound races in all weather conditions, and too much or too little rainfall can often lead to a bad racing surface, which can be a cause of many problems.

Furthermore, in a trial or race there may be up to seven other competitors all bumping and bustling to get round the track. When you consider the speed at which the greyhound travels it is quite understandable that bumps, trips and falls caused by other competitors in a race will inevitably lead to all manner of injuries.

The field or coursing dog has a host of different problems to contend with. Underfoot the ground surface is often undulating and uneven, it may be stony, or spiky with stubble straw, or clogged with mud. The hare is also a cunning creature and will often lead the dog a merry dance, turning and dodging and forcing it to turn on a sixpence when in close pursuit; in open-field coursing it may run the dog ragged over several fields, and this can also lead to metabolic problems if the dog is under-conditioned.

The Scale of Injuries

It is important that the handler realizes the vast scale of the injuries that the greyhound may sustain, and the difference in degree of those injuries. Take, for example, a muscle injury, where the varying degrees of damage may be identified as follows:

- Localized inflammation or soreness.
- A pull: depending on which muscle is pulled, it can affect how the dog performs; it can also be significant in how it affects other injuries.
- A tear in the muscle sheath.

- A thickening or a pull to the connective tendon of the muscle.
- A minor tear of the muscle, or a minor disruption of the muscle fibres and surrounding sheath.
- A small or medium tear to the actual muscle.
- A serious tear: the muscle will have haemorrhaged, and blood will be present around the damage.

Indeed within these actual groups there can be different degrees of that sort of damage, depending on which muscle is involved. It must also be understood that each group will need a different level of treatment and time off racing to deal with the injury. For example, localized muscle soreness can be neutralized with simple massage techniques, but tearing of the muscle or its fascia may well require much more aggressive therapy that needs to be prescribed by your veterinarian.

Misconceptions

There are several misconceptions about injuries, especially the minor ones. A greyhound can be running well and may even be winning races, even though it is still carrying a minor injury. To say that it is lame could be seen as an exaggeration, but the fact is that it is still injured, and if the trainer continues to run it, the risk of further injury is increased immensely. If the injury is a minor pull or strain, with ten to fourteen days' rest and with the appropriate treatment the dog may be prevented from developing a far more serious injury.

Dogs don't have to be walking lame to be lame; in fact with the majority of injuries a dog will rarely walk lame – even with a serious tear to the shoulder or gracalis muscle, it will only walk lame for a day or two. Dogs that are walking lame for more than a few days will have a foot, a bone or a ligament problem: muscle problems don't cause prolonged lameness.

For the novice trainer, or indeed any trainer, it is important to detect the minor injuries in their earliest form, and to correctly diagnose and get them treated, because not only will this stop the injury itself deteriorating, it will also prevent the dog from acquiring further, and far more serious, secondary injuries.

This issue of primary and secondary injuries is rarely recognized. However, I think it is important that any trainer, novice or not, should get some understanding of the basics of it.

TYPES OF INJURY

There are four types of physical injury: muscle, tendon, ligament and bone, and it is important that the handler has some understanding of how the greyhound's muscular and skeletal systems work. In this chapter I will explain a little about each area, and how and what he needs to be looking for.

Muscles

The muscle system is very complex, and although the trainer doesn't need to know the

veterinary science behind the anatomy of the dog, some basic information will help in understanding how injuries occur. Basically there are three types of muscle in the body: cardiac (muscles of the heart), smooth (muscles of the organs, glands, spleen) and the skeletal muscles. From an injury point of view we are only interested in the skeletal muscles.

The skeletal muscles of the dog will make up about a third to a half of the animal's total bodyweight, with the musculature often being split into two groups: the superficial muscles and the deep muscles. While all the superficial muscles can be felt or palpated, a large part of the deep muscle tissue is concealed under layers of other tissue. However, injuries still occur in these muscles even though they are difficult to detect.

Each muscle is made up of thousands of muscle fibres and is encased by a thin tissue known

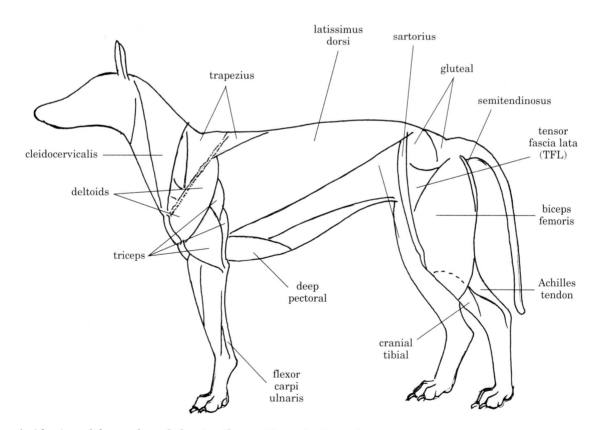

A side view of the greyhound showing the most important muscles.

79

as a sheath or muscle fascia. Although every muscle is covered by its own sheath, there are many more layers of thin tissue or fascia that fuse together and keep each muscle in place; in certain areas there can be several layers of this muscle fascia. Like the actual muscles, any fascia is open to trauma.

Each individual muscle has its own attachment to a bone or cartilage, some by a tendon or cord-like attachment while others have a more direct muscular or fleshy attachment. The muscles themselves interconnect between bones, and it is the contraction and relaxation of the muscles that extends and flexes each joint.

When dealing with muscle injuries there are two factors that must be considered.

Firstly, there are several sites that commonly become injured – the shoulder, the hip, the tensor fascia lata (or TFL), to name but a few, are areas that frequently sustain problems. However, to get a full picture of the dog's muscular state it is important that the trainer concentrates not only on the usual or most common injury sites, but he should make sure that all of the musculature is palpated to check for any damage so as to rule out any possible injuries. Learning how to feel and palpate the whole of the dog's muscular structure will enable you to find injuries you probably never thought existed.

Secondly, there are varying degrees of damage that the muscles may sustain. The muscles are made up in such a way that they can tear in all different shapes, sizes and lengths; they can tear in the belly of the muscle, at its edges or at an attachment. There may also be damage to the muscle fascia or sheath, or the sheath alone may be damaged. While serious damage is fairly easy to detect, it is the minor pulls and strains, the muscle spasms and the tense, tight, inflamed and sore muscles that can be elusive.

Serious tears in the muscles will usually make the tissue feel soft and doughy; by comparing a torn and a healthy muscle you will easily feel the difference, because it will feel as if the muscle has collapsed. Bruising and swelling is likely to accompany the damage, though it may sometimes take a day or two to emerge. Due to the softness of the tissue in its earliest stage the tear may not be detectable, but as the tear fibres up and the swelling subsides it will become easier to feel.

Smaller tears to the muscles will not have the same effect as the serious tears; swelling and bruising rarely accompany these injuries, and their presence is a little harder to detect. However, a soft spot or a soft area around the injury is usually evident, but the tear will still feel soft for a few days. When the injury has started to fibre up there are several ways in which the damage may appear: it may feel like a small line, like a thick piece of cotton or a rough cut sat in the muscle, or a knot like a small scar in the muscle, or a small pea that sits in the muscle tissue.

A minor tear to a muscle may be as small as a couple of millimetres in length, and these tears are impossible to detect if you don't palpate the muscle correctly. They are often situated around the borders of the muscle, and feel like a very small knot or cut in the tissue fibres. While their presence and relevance could easily be overlooked, it must be understood that depending on the location of these little tears, they can nonetheless have a detrimental effect on the dog's performance.

Like the muscles, the sheaths and intramuscular tissue are also susceptible to varying degrees of damage. Large tears in the sheath may be as long as 3 or 4cm in length – indeed, depending on the location and shape of these tears you may well be able to place one or two fingers in the torn sheath. Smaller, finer tears may also occur on the belly of the muscle; these feel like a thin piece of cotton sitting on top of the muscle. While sheath tears do occur on the belly of the muscles, the majority of the damage will be in the intramuscular fascia or channel between two adjacent muscles. Like the minor muscle tears, the relevance of the sheath tear may well be underestimated, and depending on the location of the tear it is likely that the dog is underperforming.

The muscles of the greyhound are very susceptible to minor pulls and strains, and this type of injury is extremely common. However, it is important to note that these injuries are not commonly recognized by the handler and frequently go undetected. Several muscles in the greyhound commonly become pulled: these include the lower neck, the trapezius, the hip, the TFL and the sartorius (whip) muscle. When injured in this way the muscle will have a much softer and thicker feel to it than it should, and in some places a soft swelling can be felt when the muscle is stroked or patted.

This type of muscle damage may not cause the dog a great deal of discomfort under palpation, and you may also find that depending on the location, the dog's performance has not deteriorated. However, if these injuries go unnoticed and untreated, there is a strong chance that further and probably more serious problems will develop.

Tendons

The tendon is the tough tissue that attaches some of the musculature to the bones. Like the muscles, the tendons are open to varying degrees of trauma, identified as a pull or a strain, a tear, or a tear at the attachment of the tendon. Swelling and thickening along the length of the tendon will probably be evident, regardless of the type of tendon injury the dog has sustained, and until this swelling has subsided the location of the damage is likely to be disguised by the enlarged tissue. When the swelling has dispersed you will be able to get a good feel of the injured tendon; damage to the attachment will probably leave a tender thickening where the tendon joins the bone.

A strained tendon and a torn tendon may well have similar characteristics, however when the tendon has been torn there is a good chance you will be able to detect the tear, which may feel like a knot or a small lump in the tendon. When the tendon is pulled or strained it will have a soft thickening to it; this thickening can sometimes be very slight, but early detection and treatment of the problem could save the dog from a potentially serious injury.

Ligaments and Joints

Nearly all the important joints in the dog's skeletal structure are known as synovial joints, where the join between two bones is contained in a bag called a capsule, reinforced by a series of tough elastic fibres known as ligaments. The inner lining of the capsule is known as the synovial membrane, and gives off synovial fluid. This fluid plays a major role in the health of the joint, because when it is combined with the smooth, shiny cartilage at the end of each bone it creates an effortless, gliding movement in the joint. The two bones of the joint will barely touch because they are cushioned and just held apart by the synovial fluid – the bones will slip and slide over one another while the pressure of the joint is maintained by the natural tension of the ligaments. The synovial fluid is important because not only does it supply the joint with nutrients, it also flushes away waste products from the joint, which is critical if the dog sustains an injury to the area.

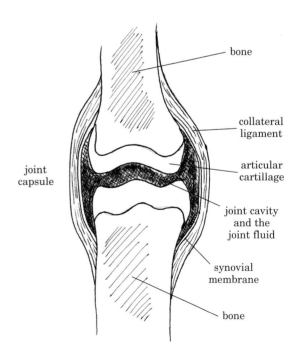

The structure of a joint.

Serious damage to a joint is usually easy to detect because the dog is likely to be lame for several days regardless of the location of the injury, there will be a strong possibility of swelling around the affected joint, and there will also be pain on flexion of it. However, mild and very mild sprains to the joints are not so easy to detect, and this can often lead to the sprain going unnoticed, and therefore the risk that it may progress into a far more serious problem.

Bones

Although serious bone damage such as a break or a fracture will be diagnosed at the track by the veterinarian, there is always a strong chance that a minor chip or a hairline fracture will go unnoticed. It is often the following morning after the run that the dog will show signs of lameness or discomfort, and it is during this post-race examination that such injuries are detected.

Due to its vagueness the hairline fracture is probably one of the hardest injuries to detect. They are most commonly associated with the metacarpal bones but the presence of very small fractures could well be found anywhere in the greyhound's structure. In most cases an opposing pressure placed across the bone or a slight pressure on the location of the damage will cause the dog some discomfort. Minor chips can often be felt as small lumps on the bone's surface; the wrist and hock joints are common sites for this type of injury but unless you learn how to feel the structure of these joints you will struggle to pick up these types of injury.

Sesamoid Bones

The sesamoid bones are found in some tendon or joint capsules, and they have three important functions: they protect the tendons as they pass over bony surfaces, they increase the surface area for the attachment of the tendons, and they direct the passage of the tendon across the joint. Each sesamoid bone is attached to the joint by a series of ligaments, which, like the actual bones, are open to trauma.

Most of the sesamoid bones are very small and are found in the toe joints: they are not much bigger than a pin head. The largest sesamoid bone is the knee cap or patella, but there are several other sesamoid bones situated in the wrist and the back of the knee.

Damage to the sesamoid bones in the toe joints is the most common problem, but although fractures of these bones do occur, the more likely problem is damage to the supporting ligaments. If any swelling is evident an X-ray should be taken to rule out bone damage.

THE EXAMINATION OF INJURIES

It is essential that every greyhound is examined the day after a race and, if it has not run very well, I would suggest that a second follow-up examination is necessary before it is run again. It must be noted that small tears and soft spots in the muscles are especially difficult to detect in their earliest form, so when examining a dog the morning after a race it can sometimes be difficult to detect certain injuries; but after a few days the change in the musculature can make these injuries much easier to detect.

For a novice the most important thing about injuries is to learn some good methods that can help you detect any problems that your dog might have. I have seen accomplished vets and trainers whose ideas on detecting injuries leaves a lot to be desired. Having a good knowledge of injuries cannot be learned overnight; indeed it can take many years of practice to achieve a true understanding of the injuries that the greyhound may sustain.

When carrying out an examination there are three good techniques that can be employed to help with the detection of any injuries: these are observation, palpation, and extension, flexion and rotation of the joints. These methods all have positive and negative attributes depending on the dog and the area being checked. However, by using a combination of all three techniques there is a good chance you will detect most injuries.

Standing at arm's length and observing the greyhound's musculature and bone structure can be a productive method of detecting injuries or problems.

Observation

Because the greyhound is short-haired and has a well-pronounced musculature, it is much easier to pick up any problems. Careful observation is often the best path to finding several injuries, and the size and shape of the limbs and muscles can be a good indication of damage or injury. Just by observing the dog closely you can often find areas of swelling or bruising that are often missed.

A good starting point is to watch the dog trot back and forth at various speeds, checking for any abnormalities in its gait (walking action). It should be noted that dogs with muscular problems rarely walk lame for more than a day or two. After watching the dog trot, it can be

beneficial to let it stand for a couple of minutes and just observe it from a distance, looking for any abnormalities in its stance; for example, is it standing straight? Is it bearing weight equally on all four limbs? Then come closer to the dog and squat down at arms' length to check its front and back end.

Examine each muscle, tendon and joint for any difference in size or shape; sometimes the change can be very slight, so it is important to look closely. A good and easy example of an injury found in this way would be a badly torn gracalis muscle; as you lift the tail to observe the gracalis, there will be a marked change in the size and shape of the muscle. A much harder injury to spot would be a very minor swelling along the Achilles tendon, which could be the result of a pull in the calf muscle or the Achilles tendon.

Palpation

Palpation is basically the touching and feeling of the greyhound's body structure so that you can detect any damage it might have sustained. Learning how to incorporate the various palpation techniques into your examination will help you learn how to detect many injuries that often go unnoticed. It must be understood that sticking your thumbs into the dog's musculature until it yelps in pain is not a clear indication of an injury, and it is important that you learn how to feel the damage that has occurred to the tissue or bone so you can differentiate between the varying degrees of trauma. However, when palpating the dog's structure, it is not always sufficient to just feel the tissue or bone: the use of different levels of fingertip pressure will increase your ability to detect different types of injury.

When carrying out an examination it is important to try and run your hands over all the musculature and bones that can be felt. And while all the superficial muscles can be palpated, it is possible to feel some of the deeper musculature by relaxing the limb and rolling the musculature between the fingers and thumb.

Identifying how the different injuries feel is one of the first things the handler needs to learn; while the serious muscle tears are easily felt in both their fibrous and soft doughy state, the minor tears to the muscles and sheaths are much more difficult to detect. Lightly rolling your fingertips around the individual muscles will give you a much better chance of feeling any damage to the muscle sheaths or fascia. It is a good idea to try to feel each individual muscle as you work from head to toe; this is where a little knowledge of the anatomy comes in handy. Use your fingers to work lightly over the belly and then round the borders of each muscle, then work over the muscle several times, increasing the pressure until you feel you have investigated the whole muscle. You will find that with practice you will work over the dog quite swiftly, because large areas of musculature such as the neck and back are felt over whole, and not as single muscles, as are the limbs.

While some injuries are detected through rolling your fingers and thumbs around the muscles, other injuries are better felt by stroking the muscle. When feeling for soft and

Use the tip of your thumb to feel gently across a muscle such as the thigh; then you can detect any slight changes in the muscle tissue. This could be anything from a tearing of the muscle or sheath to a soft spot or pull in the muscle.

pulled muscles, soft spots or minor muscle inflammation, by gently and slowly stroking over the muscle several times with your fingertips you should be able to get a better feel of the tissue. By comparing both muscles together – for example, both hips – you should be able to feel any difference in the texture or feel of the muscle.

What is most important to note is that when you stroke muscles, or run a tendon between your finger and thumb, you can often get a much better feel of the tissue when the pressure used is very, very slight. The small lumps and bumps or changes in the tissue texture will be smoothed out and become undetectable if you use too heavy a touch.

Feeling the bones and joints is basically the same as feeling the muscles, but when running your fingers over the bones you will only need to use a light pressure. Gently stroking the bones or rolling your fingers over them will help you detect any minor lumps or bumps; these minor bumps are sometimes not much bigger than a pin head, but if they are recent injuries they will be sore under increased finger pressure. They are often the result of a hairline fracture or very minor bone chip, so it is important that they are detected and treated,

as a wrong diagnosis could have serious consequences. It must also be noted that when feeling the metacarpal and metatarsal bones the thickness of the bone should be checked, as damage to the fifth metacarpal on the nearside leg can often result in a thickening of the bone.

When feeling the joints of the wrist and hock it can be beneficial to work them slowly back and forth as you do so; as well as minor bumps you are also feeling for any swelling around the joints. When feeling these bones it is also important to notice how pronounced they feel; this is because any mild swelling over the joint will leave the bones feeling less pronounced and slightly smoother.

Flexion, Extension and Rotation

When carrying out an examination it is usually best to spend a few minutes simply observing the dog before you carry out any hands-on evaluation.

When flexing, extending and rotating each joint not only should you check for any pain or discomfort, but also for the range and the smoothness of the motion, which are of equal importance. The range of motion is basically full extension to full flexion of a joint, and when checking this you are looking for any

Extend the offside shoulder not only to check for pain or discomfort in the supporting triceps muscles, but also to check the range of motion of the joint.

Flex the offside shoulder to check the range of motion, and to check for any pain or discomfort of the affected deltoid muscles.

restricted movement or shortfall on full extension or flexion. When checking the smoothness you are feeling for any resentment on motion, or any grinding of the joint.

Some trainers and vets seem to rely heavily on the flexion and extension of the joints to detect injuries, but although this is a vital part of the examination, many minor muscle problems will almost definitely be missed. It must be understood that not every muscle will be placed under the right kind of pressure, and many of the minor problems will not be serious enough to cause the dog any discomfort.

For example, when the shoulder is extended, the long head triceps becomes tight, and any serious problem will cause discomfort;

however, the lateral head of the triceps will have little pressure placed across it, and any damage will not show up. On the positive side, however, any damage to the deep musculature may well be picked up, even though there may be no sign of damage either to be seen or felt. Any problems to the joints are also detected much more easily, and you can also evaluate the health of that joint.

It is necessary to combine all three techniques in order to achieve a complete evaluation of the dog.

PRIMARY AND SECONDARY INJURIES

To put it in the simplest terms, a primary injury is a minor injury that may well affect the greyhound's gait (running action) while racing. This influence on the dog's running action can often result in a more serious secondary injury.

Primary injuries are often low key injuries such as tight, pulled or sore muscles, minor tearing of a muscle or sheath, or a minor spinal problem. Secondary injuries are usually much more serious, such as high-grade trauma to the muscles, tendons or ligaments and joints.

Depending on the situation and the severity of a primary injury, the greyhound may nevertheless be performing well and even winning races; in fact its performances can often lead to a misconception of its actual physical condition. It is quite feasible for a dog to race over a sustained period of time before the minor injury deteriorates, or a subsequent and more serious injury occurs.

On examination it is often found that a dog with a serious injury has more than one primary injury. This is because over a period of time a small niggling injury may cause two or three other niggling injuries. These injuries are a problem because the dog will automatically throw its weight to compensate for, or to ease the pressure off an injured limb, especially when it becomes tired or fatigued. This shifting or compensating of weight will inevitably place extra stress on other unsuspecting muscles and joints, with the result often being a serious injury.

The first problem for a trainer is the detection of a secondary injury. These injuries are usually easy to identify, but if the trainer rarely checks his dogs, even these can go unnoticed. Common examples of these would be a badly torn shoulder, gracalis, or tensor fascia lata (TFL), or a badly sprained wrist or hock.

The second and most important problem for a trainer is the recognition of a primary injury or injuries, as these can be elusive and difficult to feel. Due to their nature their existence could easily be questioned; indeed, a novice trainer may well have problems finding such injuries. Nevertheless, the importance of identifying these minor primary injuries is often overlooked, and it should be appreciated that the detection and treatment of some of them could well prevent the greyhound sustaining a serious injury, or could greatly reduce the chance of a recurrence in many of the secondary injuries.

For example, an injury such as a tight muscle or a spasm may well settle down of its own accord while a dog is being rested or treated for another injury. However, when the dog returns to the track the untreated tight muscle will quickly become sore, and the outcome is usually the recurrence of the main injury. Common examples of a primary injury would be soreness in the trapezius and the cervical-thoracic (c-t) junction, a pulled hip, a pulled sartorius, or a pulled tensor fascia lata.

PRIMARY INJURIES

As already discussed, primary injuries are generally mild injuries that are elusive and difficult to detect, and because of this their existence could easily be questioned. For the novice handler this type of injury will be very hard to locate, but with a little guidance he will have the opportunity to improve his skills. It is important that the novice at least appreciates the relationship between primary and secondary injuries.

The Hip

The hip muscle is important in its relationship to the dog's speed and performance. As a major part of the driving force that powers the dog, any damage to the hip can greatly affect its performance. The early pace or fast-starting greyhound will have a tendency to lose a metre or two of pace to the first bend, while the strong finishing or long-distance greyhound will tend to lose his powerful finish or will generally run badly. As well as causing poor performance, the hip injury is a strong candidate for becoming a primary injury because the greyhound that is carrying any sort of damage to the hip is likely to have another injury not too far away.

The hip is made up of four main muscles: the gluteus profundus, the gluteus medius, the gluteus superficialis and the piriformis muscle. All four are involved in the extension of the hip joint, but the gluteus profundus and the piriformis are deep muscles concealed beneath the medius and the superficialis. These deep muscles can't be palpated due to their origin, so any damage would have to be considered through the extension and flexion of the hip.

The gluteus medius is a thick muscle partially covered by the gluteus superficialis; these muscles can be easily observed and palpated. Damage to these two muscles and the fascia is common, and pulls and tears frequently plague the dog's hip muscles, but these injuries are not always recognized.

The pulled hip is a frequent injury in the greyhound's career. When comparing the hips, the pulled hip will appear larger than its counterpart and the muscle will feel softer. Using the fingertips, gently stroke the hip muscles the way the coat runs, and compare how they feel. Sometimes by gently patting or tapping the muscles with your fingertips you can see how one muscle is firm while the other is softer or even has a jelly-like feel to it. Squatting directly behind the dog will also give a good perception of how the muscle looks – though be aware that the hip muscle often becomes wasted when the hind leg becomes injured, so if the hips are of unequal size it

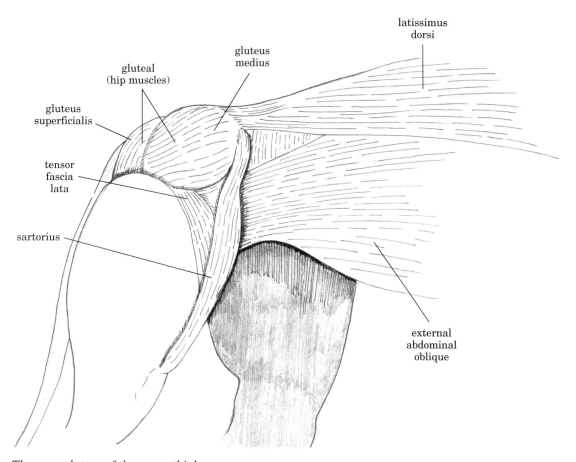

The musculature of the upper thigh.

must be established which hip is the problem. The hip should also be palpated to rule out any tears.

Tearing in the muscle of the hip is common, and is usually seen in the gluteus medius – though the damage could be considered to be somewhat inferior when compared to the often serious muscle damage seen in the shoulder, the tensor facia lata or the gracalis. While a fresh tear may cause a slight swelling or a puffiness of the muscle, a long-term tear may well have caused the muscle to waste or wither. When examining the hip you need to roll your fingers around the muscle with varying degrees of pressure to establish whether there is any damage to the muscle or its fascia.

The wasted or withered hip is again a fairly common problem. When squatting behind the dog the small hip is generally easy to see, but minor wastage can be more difficult to detect. When feeling the hip you should be able to detect a bony notch that belongs to the sacrum: when stroking the fingers gently over the notch, check how defined it feels or how much muscle is covering the notch. The difference in the thickness of the muscle covering the notch is likely to be minimal, and will only be distinguished with a gentle touch. When the hip muscle becomes wasted the notch can be felt that bit more easily due to the slight lack of muscle covering it.

However, it should be considered that the damage is not always in the hip. When detecting

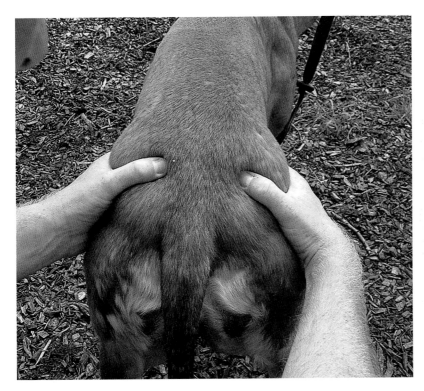

By using your finger and thumbs you can feel the hip muscles to check for any damage; while tearing is not always that common, a pull to the hip muscle happens frequently.

a withered or small hip it is wise to carry out a full and meticulous examination of the hind leg – deterioration of the hamstring, gracalis and calf may also be affected as the dog compensates and proceeds to underuse the leg.

The Tensor Fascia Lata (TFL)

Like most of the muscles, the TFL is susceptible to a varying degree of damage and like its neighbour, the hip, it frequently becomes pulled. These minor pulls will generally occur on the off side and will often accompany a pulled hip. When standing over the dog and looking down vertically at the TFL, the muscle will appear larger than its counterpart.

When the muscle is rolled between finger and thumb it will feel softer but thicker; however, no tears will be evident. This type of injury is not uncommon, and like the hip, a pulled TFL is a likely candidate for being a primary injury; it is quite common to see a dog with a wrist or a shoulder problem to have this sort of injury.

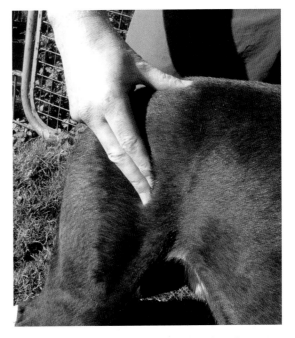

Rolling the TFL between finger and thumb is a technique used to find tears in and around the muscle and the connective tissue.

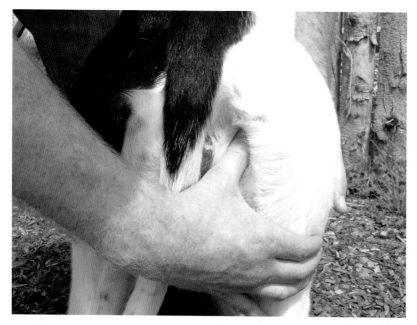

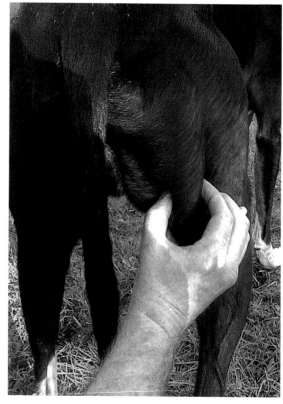

The thumb can be used to feel around the edges and deep into the muscle belly of the semimembranosus muscle. Tearing here can have a negative effect on how the greyhound performs, but is an injury that often goes unnoticed.

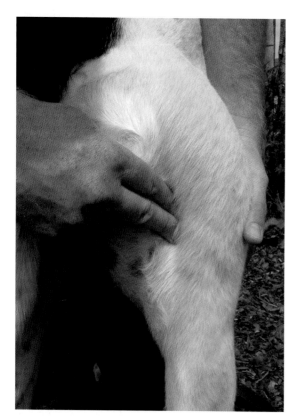

The fingers can be used to feel along the intramuscular tissue that runs between the gracalis and the semitendinosus muscles. Large tears to the fascia are not uncommon in this area.

Semimembranosus and Semitendinosus muscles

The semimembranosus and the semitendinosus are the two muscles that can be felt between the thigh and the gracalis. Most of the semimembranosus is concealed underneath the thigh and the gracalis and cannot be felt; the tissue we are interested in is at the top of the muscle and can be felt in a small triangular shape. Damage to the semimembranosus often occurs deep in the muscle's border to the gracalis; tearing of the fibres can usually be felt in a horizontal fashion, but care should be taken when palpating deep in the muscle channels. These deep tears can be difficult to detect, especially in their earliest form; however, their existence can have a detrimental effect on the dog's performance.

The semitendinosus muscle can be felt between the gracalis and the thigh; although damage to the belly of the muscle is unusual, there can be a lot of tearing of the intramuscular fascia or sheaths that can be felt in the channels between the neighbouring muscles.

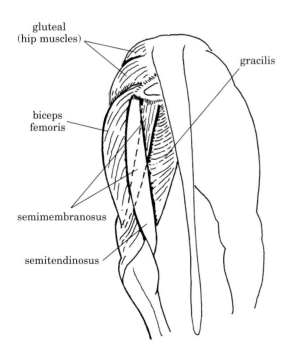

The position of the main muscles of the upper leg.

These tears or holes in the fascia can often be quite large; indeed, some of them are big enough to fit a thumb or finger end. Surprisingly, while they can easily be felt, they don't always cause the greyhound too much loss in performance; however, it is quite common to find an injury like this in a dog that has just sustained a far more serious injury – so these are often seen as primary injuries due to the way they lead to other injuries.

The Neck

When checking the musculature of the neck you must consider its complexity. It may feel as if there are just one or two large muscles, but there are in fact several layers of muscle and fascia, both superficial and deep.

It is important to flex, extend and rotate the neck to find some of the deep muscular or joint problems that are too concealed to be palpated. Firstly, elevate the head so that the dog's nose points upwards. Then push the head downwards, and bring the nose into the chest. Next, bring the head round to each side so that the nose touches the ribcage. Any pain, tension or lack of range of motion is likely to be a good indication of a problem in the neck area. If this problem is deep you are unlikely to feel it, but any damage to the superficial muscle or fascia may be detected.

Continuing the examination of the neck, you should look for any swelling or wasting of the musculature. Swelling can sometimes be seen around the base of the neck, though mostly on one side; by stroking both sides of the base of the neck you should feel for any difference, however slight.

Next, check the alignment of the head. To do this, stand over or straddle the dog, and place your left hand behind its ears at the top of the neck, and your right hand under its muzzle. Lift the muzzle upwards so that the nose points up vertically. What you are looking for is any deviation of the head: if it doesn't come up straight and moves off to the left or right, this is an indication of a problem in the axis or atlas vertebrae (the top two cervical vertebrae in the neck); it will often need the hands of a

By rotating the head round to the left the muscle tissue down the right side of the neck becomes tight. In this state it becomes much easier to feel for any damage; rippling or pulling of the tissue is fairly common.

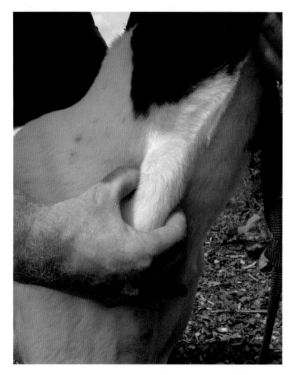

The cleidocervicalis muscle is a muscle of the neck that is regularly pulled; a thickening of the tissue is usual, but tears can sometimes be evident. This muscle is often overlooked, but it can be important in the role of primary and secondary injuries.

chiropractor to put these right. This type of injury is not that common but can sometimes be found in greyhounds that have had a serious fall or accident.

Using your fingers, you can now start palpating. First you will be able to see and feel a clearly visible line running directly down the centre of the neck. Start by feeling down this line with your thumbs in a slow, rubbing motion, working your way down the neck; small tears can occur anywhere along this line, though they will often be found around the lower portion of the neck. As you reach the base of the neck you may need to take a slightly deeper contact as you feel around the inside of the shoulder blades. These tears can be very small, not much bigger than 2mm in length, but they can often be very sore.

Then place your left hand around the head or muzzle and gently bring the head round to the left; you don't need to bring the nose all the way round to the shoulder, but you need to bring it far enough round to tighten the neck muscles on the right side. Gently stroke the musculature on the off (right) side of the neck with the fingers; the muscle should be firm and smooth, and like this it is easier to feel for any damage. If the muscle or fascia are pulled or strained, a rippling effect like tiny waves may be felt. This is not a serious problem, but the muscle should be treated until it returns to its normal smooth state.

With the muscle held like this it is also easier to feel any tears, knots or holes in the muscle fascia or sheath.

While tears can be felt anywhere in the neck, there is one particular spot that is often injured: down the side of the neck, around the base on either side, is a small, soft indentation about the size of your thumb end, which frequently becomes torn. Tears in this area will feel like a thin piece of tight string lying in the same direction as the muscle (diagonally head to neck). The length and thickness of the tear will vary.

The cleidocervicalis is the muscle that runs down the front of the neck to meet the shoulder joint, and it is important to feel it for any thickening down its length. By comparing both muscles together between your fingers and thumbs it becomes easier to identify any thickening.

The C-T Junction and the Trapezius
The cervical-thoracic junction – or the c-t junction, as it is commonly known – and the trapezius comprise a really important area in the greyhound. Many foreleg injuries are an indirect result of soreness in and around the c-t junction and the trapezius. Although both these areas may stand alone as individual injuries, it is often the case that when the c-t junction becomes sore it doesn't take long for the surrounding area to tighten up, usually resulting in soreness in the trapezius. **Keeping this whole area injury free will greatly reduce the chances of your dog sustaining serious front-end problems or any recurrences of older injuries.**

It must also be considered that when one area of the back becomes sore or injured, it is not long before another area of the back might also start experiencing soreness. When a problem such as the c-t junction goes unnoticed for a long period of time, often the lower back, mid back or both become sore as well. This soreness can often become deep-seated over a long period of time, and may well plague the dog for the whole of its career if it is not given any proper attention.

The problem for the dog is that as he is rested from racing with an injury such as a shoulder or wrist injury, then the back problem will appear to settle down. But this can be a misconception, because when the dog returns to the track the soreness in the back will gradually return, and will often result in the dog breaking down again.

The c-t junction is the joint between the seventh cervical vertebra and the first thoracic vertebra, and it is the most commonly injured vertebral joint, in part due to its range of motion. As with any joint, the greater the range of motion, the more susceptible that joint is to damage.

To check the c-t junction, first place your thumbs between the shoulder blades and the spinous process, and check for any pain as you apply a slow downward pressure. Then place your left hand on the muzzle of the dog and rotate it partially to the left; place your right thumb between the left shoulder blade and the spinous process, and apply a small rightward cross-pressure on to the spinous process to check for any pain or discomfort. Then rotate the head to the right and check the right side of the spinous process.

In its earliest form there is likely to be merely discomfort on cross-pressure of the joint, but over time it will become more and more painful. In its most progressed form the dog is likely to be very uncomfortable as soon as you put only marginal downward pressure with your thumbs between the shoulder blades. This kind of deep-seated soreness can often take quite a while to put right, but if the problem goes unnoticed and untreated it can affect the dog's whole wellbeing.

The trapezius muscle originates from the third cervical vertebra to the ninth thoracic vertebra, and is a broad, triangular-shaped, thin muscle. The muscle insertion is on the head of the scapula (shoulder blade) and also partially covers the shoulder blade as it

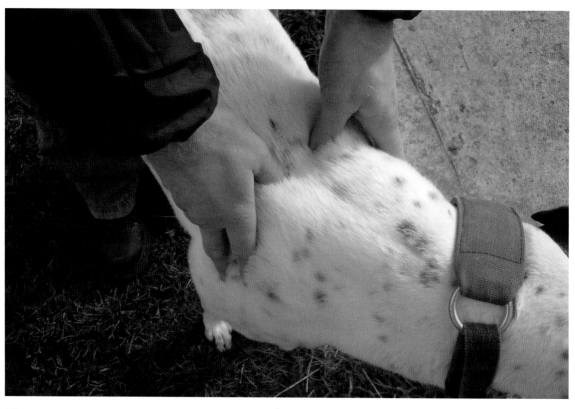

The c-t junction is one of the most important areas in the greyhound anatomy; soreness in this region can cause not only a loss in performance, but a host of further problems.

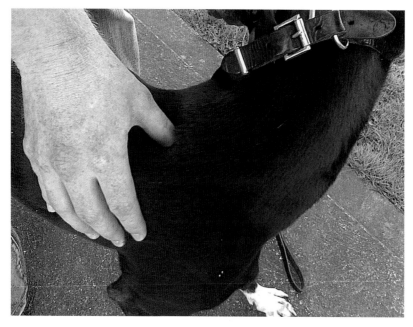

Rotating the head to the left and applying a slight opposite pressure across the c-t junction (left to right) will enable you to detect any soreness in the area. In some cases the soreness will be so deep-seated that the dog will barely be able to stand you applying any pressure. Damage to this area often goes unnoticed due to the ignorance of the handler. Damage to wrist and shoulder is often the result of this problem.

stretches over the lower neck and the upper back. The muscle's function is to draw the foreleg up and forwards.

To check the trapezius, run your first two fingers along the head of the scapula (shoulder blade) with a slight downward pressure. Any minor problem and the dog may be simply unhappy with your touch, but as the problem becomes more deep seated and sore it will dip down and totally resent your touch or any slight pressure placed on the scapula head. As you palpate the trapezius the muscle will feel tight and sore, and discomfort will be evident if any firm pressure is applied. Roll your fingers around the muscle to feel for any tearing of the muscle or its fascia; the level of pain and discomfort is often a good indication as to how serious the problem is.

To clarify what causes the pain on the shoulder blade: the trapezius attaches to the head of the scapula, and as the muscle becomes tight, the muscle pulls at the attachment causing pain under palpation. Imagine an elastic band pulled tight between two pencils: as you rotate one pencil the band twists and becomes tighter, thus shortening the distance between the pencils as they are pulled together. This is similar to the tightened muscle: the tightening at the attachment causes the soreness.

When checking the trapezius it is also important to check for any wastage of the muscle. Make sure the dog is standing square and bearing equal weight on both forelimbs when you observe and palpate the trapezius. First look for any running away of the muscle (muscle wastage); this usually occurs around the side of the muscle as you follow the natural curve off the top of the shoulder blade. In severe cases of wasting the shoulder blade will appear quite pronounced, because the withered muscle barely covers the edge of the scapula. As you palpate around the shoulder blade and gently stroke

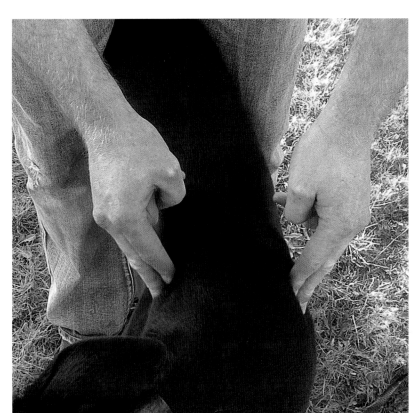

Use your index and middle finger to work along the head of the scapula to feel for any soreness. This is usually evident around the top of the scapula and is associated with a problem in the trapezius and the c-t junction.

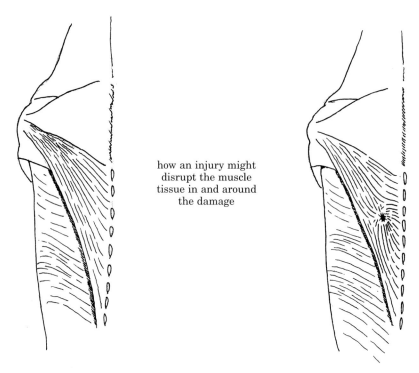

how an injury might
disrupt the muscle
tissue in and around
the damage

How a knot or tear in the musculature can disrupt the surrounding tissue.

over the trapezius muscle with the lie of the coat it should become easy to decipher any wastage.

There are two common problems that cause this muscle wastage: firstly a tear, often felt as a knot in the musculature; and secondly, a blockage can mean that the muscle is not worked effectively, so that over a period of time it wastes away. The blockage or thickened muscle can be felt between the shoulder blade and the third spinous process. By gently stroking through the gap between the spine and the shoulder blades, a hard thickening may be felt on the side of the wasted muscle. With treatment to the thickened muscle the trapezius should return to its normal state, and then as the muscle starts getting worked correctly, it should build up and in time will return to normal.

It must be noted that the torn muscle will probably always have a marked wastage, even after treatment of the problem.

The Back

Although the spine and the surrounding musculature is complicated, and indeed any region of the back may become injured, the four main problem areas that are most susceptible to injury are the four junctions with the greatest range of motion:

The skull-axis-atlas: These are the first two joints of the spine and are situated behind the skull; they are commonly known as the 'yes' and 'no' joints.

Cervical-thoracic junction: The c-t junction is situated between the shoulder blades and is the joint that joins the seventh cervical vertebra and the first thoracic vertebra.

Thoracic-lumbar junction: This is the joint between the thirteenth thoracic vertebra and the first lumbar vertebra. By counting up the seven lumbar spinous processes you should be able to locate this joint, which is midway down the back.

Lumbar-sacral junction: This is the joint between the seventh lumbar vertebra and the sacrum. This whole lower back region is a problem area.

There are thirteen thoracic and seven lumbar vertebrae that make up most of the length of the back, and it is important to check the length of these spinal vertebrae for any damage or soreness that may have occurred.

First, stand over the dog and square him up so that he stands straight, then let him relax and check that his back is straight. His spine should be straight, and should not deviate in any way or bend like a banana. If it does, this is a good indication of a problem in the back.

Next, squat beside the dog and with your finger and thumb on either side of the vertebrae, run your fingers slowly along the spine. Feel around the spinous processes and check for any swelling or localized muscle spasm, for any bones that feel off centre, or anything that feels abnormal.

Standing over the dog, now place your thumbs on either side of the spine, starting at the c-t junction and working your way down the spine to the tail. You need to use a slight downward pressure with your thumbs on each joint in a sort of gentle bouncing motion. As you work over each joint you will find that if it is healthy it will give way under the downward pressure, but as you apply pressure on a damaged joint it will probably feel stiff and may well be a little sore or painful.

To get a different perspective of any further problems you can use a cross-pressure technique. This is basically putting your left thumb on the left side of the spinous process and your right thumb on the right side of the next spinous process, and then applying a gentle cross-pressure to check for any soreness.

Starting at the c-t junction, work your way down the spine and try and check each joint – though when you reach the eighth to twelfth thoracic processes you may have a little trouble

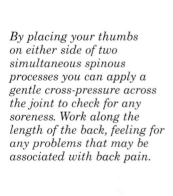

By placing your thumbs on either side of two simultaneous spinous processes you can apply a gentle cross-pressure across the joint to check for any soreness. Work along the length of the back, feeling for any problems that may be associated with back pain.

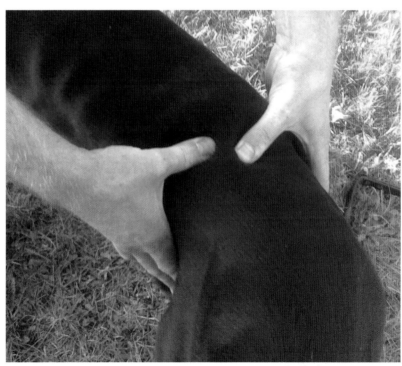

distinguishing them apart because they are so close together. Any soreness or discomfort on cross-pressure is a good indication of a problem in or around the joint.

The musculature of the back is also quite complicated, though muscle and fascia tears are not that common; nevertheless it is still important to check for any such damage. By simply stroking your fingers over the dog's back you can feel the indentations or soft spots that indicate a tear, and on feeling the injury more closely you may find that you can place a finger in a hole in the muscle fascia. In other cases you may find a knot or a thick tear in the musculature. These tears may be found anywhere down the length of the back.

If you find any problems to the neck or spine it is important that you seek advice from a veterinarian or a chiropractor.

SECONDARY INJURIES

It could be considered that the secondary injury is far more common than the primary injury, but this is only because the primary injury widely goes unrecognized. The two most common secondary injuries that the greyhound sustains are the sprained wrist and the torn shoulder, and it is important to look at these in some detail.

As well as damage to the shoulder and the wrist, there are several other injuries that frequently give the greyhound problems.

The Shoulder

A very large number of greyhounds – I would suggest a quarter to a third of all track dogs – will sustain a shoulder injury at one point or another during their racing career. Although both of the shoulders are open to damage, the offside shoulder of the racing dog becomes injured far more frequently than the nearside shoulder; this is because the extra stress placed on the offside limb as the dog negotiates a left-handed bend is enough to cause all sorts of shoulder problems for the racing dog.

If the injury is not too serious, then with correct treatment there should not be too many complications.

Several muscles make up the shoulder: there are four triceps muscles (long head,

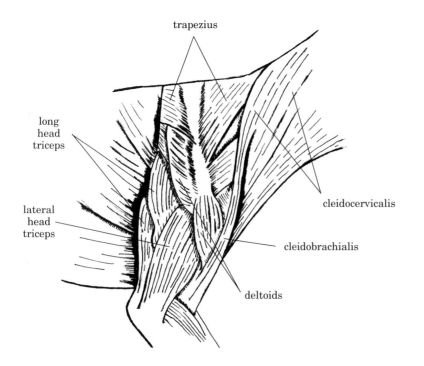

The musculature of the shoulder.

trapezius

long head triceps

lateral head triceps

cleidocervicalis

cleidobrachialis

deltoids

medial head, accessory head and the lateral head), two deltoid muscles, the brachialis, the cleidobrachialis and the infraspinatus, largely concealed by the deltoid muscles. Underneath the scapula and the shoulder lie the subscapularis, the supraspinatus, the biceps brachii, the deep pectoral, the teres major, and a small portion of the latissimus dorsi which originates on the humerus. Due to their location several of these shoulder muscles cannot be seen or palpated, which can make any injuries in these muscles difficult to diagnose.

There are two main areas of the shoulder that frequently become injured: firstly the long head triceps (often known as the monkey muscle) is open to a broad spectrum of damage. The problems here vary on a scale from minor sheath tears to serious muscular damage to both the muscle and the attachment.

Secondly, small tears frequently occur to the musculature at the base of the channel where the two deltoid muscles cross over the triceps lateral head; this injury can have a most negative effect on how the dog performs. Although

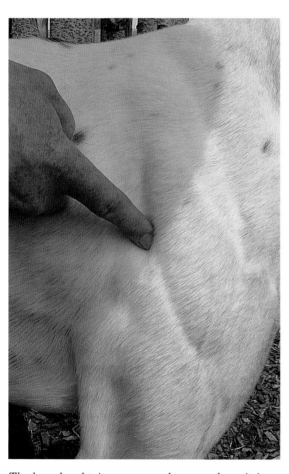

The long head triceps, or monkey muscle as it is commonly known, is a frequent cause of injury to the greyhound. This is one of the muscles where serious muscle damage can occur, but it is also a common place to find small and intricate tears. Greyhounds that swing off on the bends are usually carrying an injury to the offside shoulder.

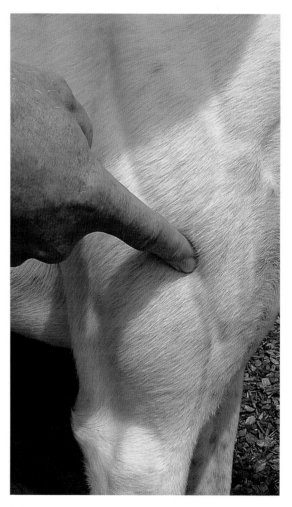

This is an area of the shoulder that frequently becomes torn, though tearing here is sometimes a little more difficult to detect due to the nature of the tear.

there are other injuries to consider in the shoulder region, these two areas are by far the most commonly affected.

When comparing shoulder injuries between track and field dogs, the field dog's are more equally spread between both the shoulders, largely because it is not bound to the same repetitive left-hand turn that plagues the racing dog – this can easily be seen in the amount of offside shoulder damage that the track dog incurs.

It must also be noted that the shoulder is a secondary injury, and as with all secondary injuries, it is therefore important to try and pinpoint the primary injury. As mentioned earlier, it can be unwise to leave a primary injury undetected and untreated, because in doing so this often leads to a reoccurrence of the secondary injury – in this case the shoulder.

When examining the shoulder, the first task is to observe both the shoulders and check for any swelling, bruising or muscle wastage – be sure to check underneath each shoulder, too.

Standing over the dog, flex and extend both forelegs and check for any stiffness or soreness in the shoulders; it is also important to check for the smoothness of the movement. Any discomfort or resistance is a good indication of a problem in the shoulder area; however, there are many different problems, including damage to the shoulder or elbow joint, to the scapula (shoulder blade) or humerus, and to the musculature.

Muscle Damage

Several muscles make up the shoulder, but the main key muscles are the deltoids and the triceps, and the intramuscular fascia that joins and lies between them. Although these are the two main muscles, it is still important that the whole of the musculature of the shoulder is felt.

Standing over the dog, first just run your hands in a gentle stroking motion over the whole of each shoulder, feeling for any difference in how they feel. Then starting at the shoulder blade, use your fingers to feel for any pain or discomfort down the underneath of the head of the scapula (shoulder blade). Any pain around the lower portion of the scapula

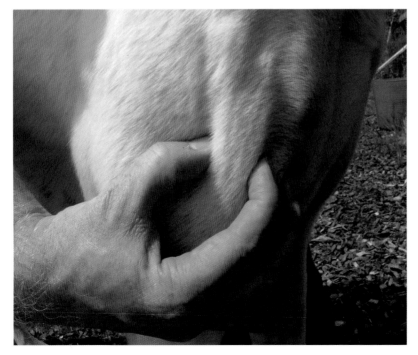

Use your finger and thumb to get a good feel of the size and shape of the lower deltoid. This muscle feels thicker when it has been pulled.

head is a good indication of a problem in the deltoid muscle.

Then come down on to the deltoid muscle and, using varying degrees of pressure, roll your fingers around the large deltoid head feeling for any puffiness or tears to the muscle or sheath. It is useful to feel both shoulders together, as this will help you to feel any changes in how the musculature feels.

Then come on to the smaller deltoid head, which feels like a short, fat, sausage-shaped muscle; it occasionally becomes pulled, and will feel puffy and slightly swollen when compared to its opposite number.

Moving on to the triceps, first feel along the channel that separates the deltoid from the triceps for any damage that may have occurred to the sheath or the triceps muscle that sits directly below the deltoid. Tears appear anywhere along the length of this channel, but again, varying degrees of pressure must be used: if you use too heavy a pressure you will not feel the small, thin sheath tears that occur regularly.

At the base of this channel, sat just inside the shoulder joint, a number of tears may be discovered to the lateral triceps head. The tears here may be deep in the muscle, and will feel like a tight, thin piece of string that will vary in length; the surrounding tissue is likely to feel soft and doughy if the injury is fresh. As mentioned earlier, tears here are frequent, and depending on the severity of the problem, the greyhound is likely to be running poorly, although the damage will rarely cause it to walk lame.

At the top of the channel is the monkey muscle, which is the top portion of the long head triceps; this muscle has a round, sphere-type feel to it, and is a common problem area. This is the muscle in the shoulder that sustains the majority of the really serious tears; in their worst form you will see a great deal of bruising and swelling along the back and underneath the shoulder, along the chest and maybe extending as far as the hind legs, and right down around the wrist and paw. The muscle will feel large, soft and doughy, and almost as if it has collapsed.

It may take a while for the swelling to disperse so that you can get a good feel of the injury; when the swelling does subside, the tears will be felt in a vertical direction as one or more thick strands of cord. In some cases the tear may feel like one big knot in the muscle.

Damage to the attachment will be felt as a thickening at the top of the muscle, where you can feel it attach to the scapula. Again the seriousness of the injury can often be determined by the amount of bruising and swelling that accompanies the damage.

Serious muscle tears like this will usually cause the dog to break down during a race and be walking lame almost straight afterwards. However, even in serious tears the dog is usually walking relatively sound within a few days. If a dog with a serious tear is still walking lame after a week, there is a strong chance it has an accompanying injury; this will probably be a joint or bone problem, so further investigation is needed.

It must also be appreciated that smaller, less pronounced tears to the monkey muscle and the fascia occur here regularly; in the muscle these will feel like a small knot, and in the fascia like a thin piece of cotton. Depending on their severity, these injuries are likely to have a progressively detrimental effect on the dog's performance. These small muscular or sheath tears can easily go undetected, and in all likelihood will lead to a much more serious problem; this may not be in the shoulder, but may be elsewhere.

The Shoulder Guider

The shoulder guider sits just inside the shoulder behind the monkey muscle. When feeling between the ribcage and the shoulder you should be able to find a thin piece of cord-like tissue that runs horizontally. When you feel this tissue it is important to feel both sides together and compare them, because it is not unusual for the offside guider to become pulled, when it will feel much tighter and thicker than the opposite guider.

Although in general this injury is not serious, there is a possibility that when the guider becomes very tight and sore the dog may well

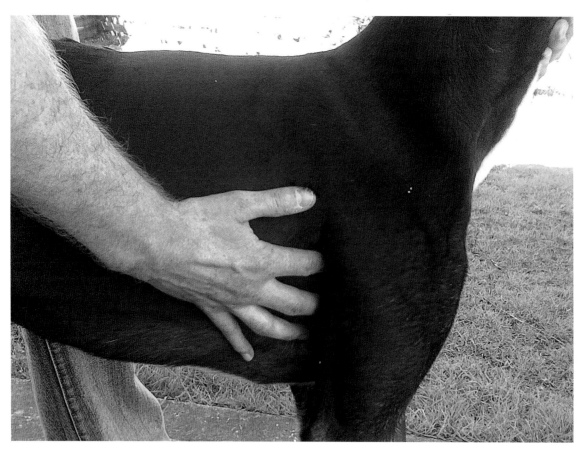

By using your index finger the guider can be felt between the ribcage and the underside of the monkey muscle. The tissue lies horizontally and can be felt like a thin piece of tight string; it is the thickness and the tightness that needs to be assessed. The offside guider is the usual problem, with the dog often running off at the turn.

drift off at the bends or struggle to hold its line. It is therefore advisable to try and return the guider to its natural state before returning the dog to the track.

Wrist Injuries

The wrist injury is the one injury that is a real nightmare for any owner or trainer. A serious wrist injury could finish a dog's career, so any damage, however mild, is of paramount significance to the greyhound.

The wrist is made up of seven bones, arranged in two rows: the radius, the ulna and the accessory carpal bone make up the upper three proximal carpal bones, while the bottom four bones make up the smaller distal carpal bones. The radius and the ulna unite the top of the wrist, while the five metacarpal bones join to the distal carpal bones, making up the lower portion of the wrist.

All the bones of the carpal joint are connected and interconnected by a vast number of ligaments that make the wrist a complicated set of joints. The carpal joint is split into three main separate joints, namely the proximal, the middle and the distal joints, which flex, extend and give lateral movement to the wrist. On top of this there is a series of intercarpal joints that join together the singular carpal bones, which further complicate the joint.

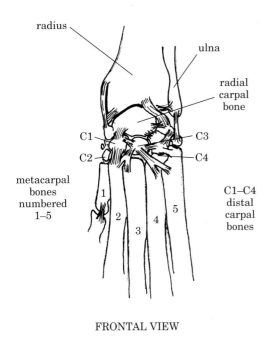

FRONTAL VIEW

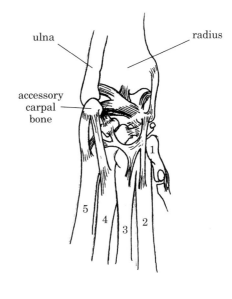

REAR VIEW

The complicated set of ligaments that hold the wrist in place.

Checking the Wrist

The complexity of the wrist seriously increases the risk of trauma, and any damage to it must be given considerable respect: many of the injuries that occur in the wrist can severely affect the greyhound's racing career, and in some cases retirement is the only option. The sheer number of bones and ligaments all compacted into such a small area can make the actual diagnosis of a wrist injury fairly difficult, so a good working knowledge of the wrist will help the trainer identify any problems that the dog may have sustained.

When checking the wrist it is best first just to observe it: a good starting point is to compare both wrists, looking for any swelling, lumps or bumps that shouldn't be there. If the dog is examined regularly then any changes will be noticed a lot more readily. While some serious damage to the joint can result in a large soft swelling over the wrist, a more chronic old injury may have a much firmer or even hard lumpy feel to it; furthermore, some

such firm lumps on the wrist can be the result of an old infection – they are more commonly seen in field dogs, but are occasionally seen in track dogs.

Next gently flex, extend and rotate the wrist, checking for any pain, restricted movement or lack of smoothness in its motion. Then flex the wrists and check for any sign of pain when they are put under increased pressure; if full flexion is achieved with no discomfort, then gently rock the wrist from side to side while it is fully flexed; this will bring different ligaments into the equation. If pain or discomfort is evident under any movement or pressure, it is important to identify the location and severity of the injury.

When pain is evident on flexion of the wrist, you should not to jump to the conclusion that the dog has a sprained wrist. While flexing the wrist a certain amount of pressure will be placed on the metacarpal bones, the accessory carpal bone and several of the muscles of the foreleg, and with this in mind it is wise to use palpation to discover the true location of the injury.

Third and most importantly, use your fingers and thumbs to feel the structure of the wrist, the accessory carpal bone, the metacarpals and the foreleg to check for any damage. When feeling the carpal bones at the front of the wrist it can help to slightly flex and extend the wrist while gently rolling your thumb over the bones. Moving the wrist like this can give you a much better feel of any changes to the bone or its supporting tissue.

After feeling the front of the wrist you need to check the accessory carpal bone, gently feeling around the bone and checking for any swelling around the whole bone, but especially the top. It is important that any swellings or bumps are picked up at an early stage.

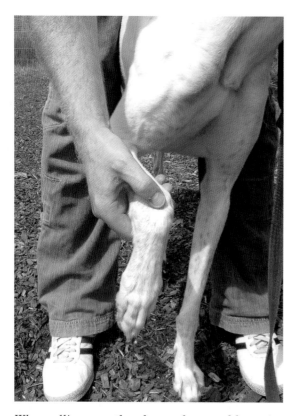

When rolling your thumb over the carpal bones it is important that the contact used is light; by applying too much pressure you will not get the desired feel of the bones.

Sprained Wrist

A sprained wrist is relatively common; what must be established is how severe the injury is. The top joint or proximal joint that lies between the radius and the radial carpal bone is the most likely candidate due to its range of motion, however, the middle carpal joint is also susceptible to damage.

When the wrist is flexed the amount of pain will give a good indication of how bad the injury may be. Severe pain on flexion, accompanied by a visible swelling, should start the alarm bells ringing and the dog should be seen by a veterinarian to rule out any possible bone damage.

A dog that experiences pain or discomfort when the wrist is fully flexed, but without any visible swelling, is likely to have a sprained wrist. A good exercise is to extend and flex the wrist back and forth, for one second each time, about ten or fifteen times, and after the last extension, flex the wrist to check for the amount of pain; if there is no pain at all the sprain is probably relatively mild. If there is little change in the amount of discomfort the sprain is probably far more serious.

Another good test is to hold the foreleg off the ground and let the wrist hang at 90 degrees, then with your fingertip very gently stroke the wrist several times until you get a good feel for the bones in the wrist. Then pick up the good wrist and repeat the process: take your time, and get a good feel for both the wrists. What you are looking for is a slight swelling over the wrist; this swelling is sometimes easy to feel, but often it can be so slight that you wonder if it is there at all. When feeling the wrist you are trying to detect how pronounced the bones feel, because the carpal bones on the injured wrist are likely to feel slightly smoother if there is a thin line of swelling beneath the surface.

Sometimes just applying pressure on flexing the wrist is not enough to test its health. But if it is rocked back and forth horizontally while flexed, then discomfort can sometimes be detected. This is often an indication of a mild sprain, which may seem irrelevant or, due to its nature, could easily be missed. If a dog is allowed to run with a minor sprain like this it will only be a matter of time before the wrist deteriorates or the dog sustains another injury as it tries to take the pressure off the injury.

Arthritis in the Wrist

Chronic or old wrist injuries have plagued many a dog's racing career – indeed, many dogs will have been retired due to arthritis in the wrist. The greyhound will often perform reasonably well, but after the race will show signs of lameness and be sore in the wrist. Over the course of the next few days the lameness and pain will subside, but the wrist is likely still to be sore under pressure from flexion. When observing and feeling the wrist there is likely to be a soft swelling over the wrist joint. Depending on the stability of the wrist and the sustained treatment from the trainer, the dog may well be raced every ten to fourteen days without a great loss in its performance. However, if the wrist is left untreated and the dog run too much, it will probably break down altogether, and will struggle to run again without being extremely lame.

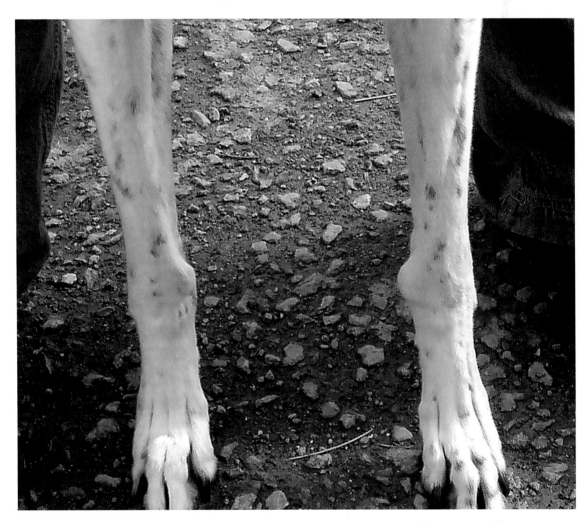

This greyhound has a clearly visible swelling on the nearside wrist; many of the wrist problems may not be this clear, but it is important that the novice learns how to spot any injuries, especially to the wrist.

Arthritis in the wrist is not uncommon, and is generally brought about by the natural wear and tear of racing. The wrist is a synovial joint, and the joint is held together by the natural tension of the ligaments and soft tissue. When trauma occurs, the flow of synovial fluid into the wrist can be disrupted and slow right down, with the result that the ligaments and tendons become dry and lose their flexibility. The bone and cartilage can become brittle, and there may even be bony changes in the wrist as the bones rub on each other because the joint has lost its natural tension.

All this aggravation in the joint can cause it to swell, and leaves the dog with restricted movement. The swollen joint can then cause stretching of the connective ligaments and soft tissue, leaving the wrist even more sore and painful. At this point any slight knock or over-exertion of the wrist can be very painful, and running the dog will cause visible lameness and pain straight after the race.

The arthritic pain in the wrist can also be caused by the chemical irritation that is a natural part of the inflammation that occurs in living tissue when it becomes damaged. The chemical substances released can irritate the nerve endings in the living tissue, which registers as pain in the joint.

Treatment of Wrist Injuries

When the greyhound is experiencing problems in the wrist such as these, the usual option is to rest the wrist and keep it still. However, while serious injuries should be rested for an initial period, too much rest can in fact have a deleterious effect and actually cause the wrist to seize up and lose mobility. Simple extension and flexion of the wrist can help pump away excess fluid, soften the thick and swollen tissue, and restore the elasticity to the joint's ligaments and surrounding tissue. Depending on how severe the pain is, movement of the joint should start off gently and then progress as it becomes less painful and tight. The health of the wrist can sometimes be remarkably improved if the trainer is willing to put in the time and effort to treat it in this way.

If a wrist injury is spotted straight after the race, it is important to get it under a cold tap immediately and to hold it there for a few minutes. For the next forty-eight to seventy-six hours the wrist can then be ice packed, or hosed off at five- or six-hour intervals.

After the initial three or four days a hot kaolin poultice can be applied to the wrist every eight hours. When changing the poultice, apply some manual therapy to help flush away any waste, and to prevent the wrist from seizing up.

I prefer to have any wrist injury inspected and injected by a veterinarian to give it the best chance of recovery. I have also had a lot of success with the use of spirit blisters; however, it is important to seek veterinary advice, as these can be potent concoctions.

The Accessory Carpal Bone

The accessory carpal bone is situated at the back of the wrist; it is supported by a number of carpal ligaments at the back and bottom of the bone, which stabilize the joint and oppose the natural tension of the flexor carpi ulnaris.

Damage to the accessory carpal bone is usually accompanied by a varying degree of swelling; how much will largely depend on the location and severity of the injury. Any fractures or breaks to the accessory carpal bone will generally be accompanied by considerable swelling around the back of the wrist, a lot of pain will be evident on flexion, and lameness is likely to be fairly severe. The problem is that severe spraining of the accessory carpal ligaments can often pose the very same symptoms as a fracture; it is therefore important to have the wrist radiographed whenever any swelling is evident to rule out any possible fractures.

When carrying out an examination of the accessory carpal bone it is important to feel around the bone for any minor swellings; these often appear at the top of the bone, but they can also be deep at the base. Minor strain to the ligaments in the back of the wrist can cause a slight swelling, but there is nearly always lameness when the accessory carpal bone is involved. Using your finger to gently feel or stroke the top of the bone, you need to compare both bones together because the damaged bone structure will feel less pronounced than its counterpart; however, this swelling can often be very minor and difficult to detect.

After feeling the wrist, check the mobility of the carpal joint with upward, downward and lateral pressure to reveal any pain or discomfort. First take the carpal bone between finger

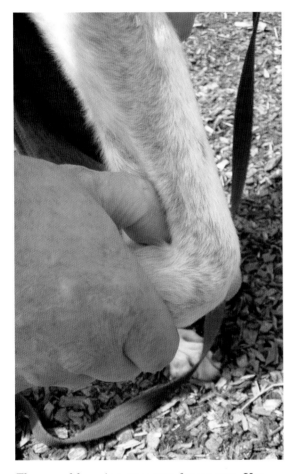

The carpal bone is a true area for concern. Use your thumb to place a gentle downward pressure on the bone, and also to feel around the carpal bone itself for any discomfort or swelling. Minor swelling is often evident at the attachment of the bone, however, this swelling is often very minor and easily missed. If a greyhound was run with a minor injury like this the outcome could well lead to a career-threatening problem.

and thumb, and with the leg lifted, gently move it from side to side. Then with the thumb above the carpal bone and the wrist slightly flexed, place a downward pressure on to the bone. Finally, with your thumb below the carpal bone, place an upward pressure on the bone. If any pain or discomfort is evident it is a clear indication of a problem to the bone or the supporting ligaments.

When feeling the accessory carpal bone there may be minor lumps or bumps that must be looked out for; these are usually very small, but when you get used to the shape of the bone they become easier to detect. Their presence is usually the result of very minor bone damage, so you need to check for any signs of discomfort around the area.

The problem with damage to the accessory carpal bone is that whether it is a minor ligament strain or a serious fracture, the injury can often end the dog's racing career. The chance of a recurrence is high, so the handler should always take the cautious approach.

The Flexor Carpi Ulnaris Muscle

The flexor carpi ulnaris is an important muscle of the foreleg. It has two bellies: the ulnar head and the humeral head, both of which attach to the accessory carpal bone by a strong tendonous attachment. The inside of the muscle cannot be felt because it is covered by the flexor digitorum superficialis; the outside of the muscle and the tendon, however, can be felt easily.

The most common problem suffered by this flexor muscle is tearing or straining of the tendon or its attachment, when swelling will be evident around the bottom of the tendon and around the top of the stopper bone. These symptoms are very similar to those of the damaged accessory carpal bone, so take particular care in diagnosis. When the swelling has subsided the damage can usually be felt as a small lump or a thickening of the tendon, either on the attachment or within the first few centimetres of tendon.

When carrying out an examination it is important to check the muscle as well as the

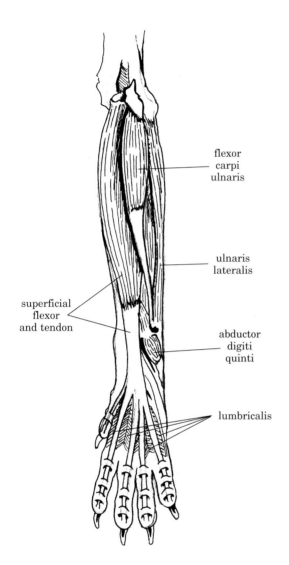

flexor
carpi
ulnaris

ulnaris
lateralis

superficial
flexor
and tendon

abductor
digiti
quinti

lumbricalis

The musculature of the foreleg.

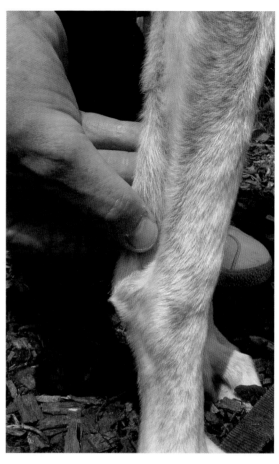

Using fingertip pressure you can feel along the length of the tendons and around the carpal bone. While some people feel it is easier to use their thumbs, others find it easier with their fingertips.

tendon: with your finger and thumb on either side of the tendon, use fingertip pressure to feel the length of the muscle and tendon. Starting at the wrist, gently feel the length of the muscle right up to the elbow, working up and down several times using weaker and stronger pressures. Damage can sometimes be found about halfway between the wrists and elbow, as very small tears in the muscle or sheath; these can be easily overlooked, but can cause problems for the dog.

The Foreleg Muscles

There are several muscles in the foreleg, which all play there own role in the flexion and extension of the wrist joint. When pain is evident on flexion of the wrist it is often concluded that that is where the damage is; however, some of the foreleg muscles have a tendonous attachment that crosses the carpal joint and ends on the front of the metacarpal bones and toes. When the wrist is flexed, these muscles and tendons become stretched, and damage to any of them will inevitably cause discomfort.

By placing your hand underneath the elbow and extending the foreleg, the muscles will contract and become more distinguished and easy to feel across the wrist. However, you may also find that when extended, the wrist does not fully extend due to damage in one of the foreleg muscles.

When the wrist is held in this tensed state, the tendons crossing the carpal joint can also be felt for any slight thickening.

The Metacarpal Bones

The metacarpal bones are the five rod-like bones that connect the toes to the wrist; like the toes, each metacarpal is numbered. Starting with the dew claw, which is number one, each metacarpal is numbered two, three, four and five working outwards or laterally. Note that if the dog has its dew claws removed, the numbering system remains the same. In the greyhound this is quite important, because metacarpal five on the nearside leg and metacarpal two on the offside leg are the two bones that are prone to damage. The meta-carpal bones are not straight, and when viewed from the side they form a sort of arch; this means that when the dog runs round a left-handed bend, its weight is placed on the outside metacarpal of the nearside and the inside metacarpal of the offside leg.

Damage to the metacarpal bones is often due to bad management on the part of the trainer. Young dogs that are run too frequently can often develop metacarpal problems due to the bones not being able to cope with the extra stress placed on them. As a young greyhound starts to run on a circular track the metacarpals are placed under a new stress that they are not used to; however, given time, the dog's own response unit will strengthen these bones to cope with the new stress. However, if the dog is run too often, the bones cannot strengthen sufficiently in the shorter time between races, which can result in damage to the metacarpals.

A common problem to the metacarpal bones is shin soreness, which is an inflammation of the surface layer of the bone. How badly it affects the dog will largely depend on the severity of the damage. The main problem with this type of injury is that if it is not picked up in its earliest form, then the damage may well develop into a hairline fracture.

When checking the metacarpals it is best to observe the bones closely to check for any swelling, which may well be minor. Then lift the wrist, and while supporting the wrist with your left hand, gently rotate or twist the foot to the left and right. The cross-pressure placed on the metacarpal bones may well cause the dog discomfort if there is any minor problem to the bones.

Then use your fingers and thumb to gently stroke over the bones to check for any minor lumps or bumps; these can be very small, and usually indicate a hairline fracture.

When feeling the bones you will sometimes find that metacarpal five on the inside leg will have a thickening to it, which can sometimes be quite prominent. The cause of this is a prolonged case of shin soreness, which has caused the bone to thicken to cope with the extra stress placed on it.

The Tensor Fascia Lata

The tensor fascia lata, or the TFL as it is commonly known, is a crucial muscle; its triangular shape makes it quite distinctive and easy to detect. The TFL borders the hip and the sartorius muscle, but the bottom of the muscle is covered by the biceps femoris or thigh. Its action is to flex the hip and extend the stifle joint, and it is a hotspot for a wide range of problems.

Like most of the muscles, the TFL is open to a varying degree of damage, and like its neighbour, the hip, it frequently becomes pulled. These minor pulls will generally occur on the offside, and will often accompany a pulled hip. When standing over the dog and looking down vertically at the TFL, the muscle will appear larger than its counterpart.

When the muscle is rolled between finger and thumb it will feel softer but thicker, but no tears will be evident. Like the hip, a pulled TFL is a likely candidate for being a primary injury, and it is quite common to see a dog with a damaged wrist or a shoulder to have this sort of an injury.

Minor tears to the TFL can have a serious effect on the dog's performance, and it is not uncommon for it to be racing many lengths below its best racing times. These minor tears to the muscle or fascia are often difficult to detect, and if they are left unresolved there is a possibility that the tear will open up the tissue into a much more severe tear. Although the dog may be running badly, it will rarely walk or trot lame. When checking the TFL it is wise to feel both sides together: starting with a gentle pressure, roll your fingers around the belly of the muscle feeling for any damage.

Tearing of the sheath may well feel like one or more small pieces of cotton sitting on the muscle surface, but as you start to increase the pressure and feel deeper into the muscle, you may well find disruption of the muscle fibres.

To get a good feel of the insertion of the muscle and its belly, stand over the dog, place your free hand on the inner thigh underneath the TFL, and gently lift the muscle. Then gently feel in the borders of the hip and whip muscles

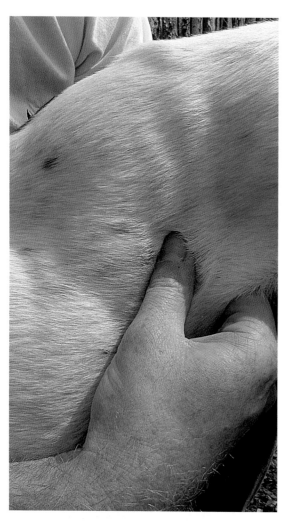

By taking the TFL muscle between finger and thumb, and rolling the muscle, you can get a good feel of any damage.

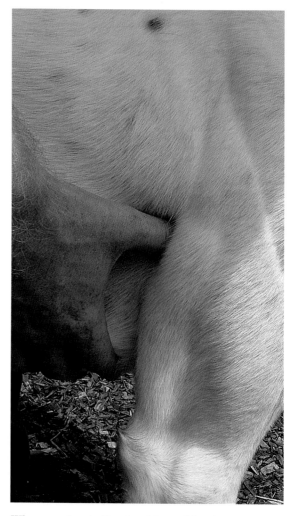

When you locate the shoulder guider (see page 101) you can use your thumb to gently roll over the tissue to feel for any changes.

that neighbour the TFL: minor tearing of the muscle's border or the adjoining fascia may be evident. These tears are often very small, sometimes not much bigger than a pin head, and while they may seem of little consequence, their existence can often cause the greyhound's performance to deteriorate badly.

Any serious tearing of the TFL is of paramount significance, as it can undoubtedly end the greyhound's racing career. Unlike the bad tears in the shoulder or the gracalis, the TFL will often have a much firmer feel and the muscle may well appear much thicker and harder, which is in complete contrast to how most muscle injuries feel.

The actual damage or tear is usually difficult to feel at first, due to the nature of the muscle's texture. The dog is likely to be very lame, swelling and bruising may be evident as far down the leg as the hock and hind feet, and the dog will feel a lot of discomfort on the slightest extension of the leg. The muscle should be ice-packed or hosed with cold water to reduce the swelling, and the dog presented to a veterinarian for examination as soon as possible. Depending on the damage, the veterinarian may be able to stitch the muscle, which, from a racing point of view, could give it a much better chance of a full recovery.

The Gracalis

The gracalis muscle is a superficial muscle that lies on the inner thigh; it is of paramount importance in relation to the greyhound's racing career. It originates from the pelvis and detaches on the fibia just below the stifle with a tendonous attachment; the latter spreads into a band of tissue that joins the semitendinosus tendon that makes up a portion of the Achilles tendon. The gracalis muscle is involved in the extension of the hip and the adduction of the thigh.

Serious trauma to the gracalis is not uncommon, and depending on the severity of the tear and the quality of the treatment, the dog's racing career may well have reached an abrupt end. However, not all damage to the gracalis is this critical, and when carrying out an examination it should always be thoroughly investigated, as minor tearing of the muscle and its fascia is fairly common.

Major tearing of the gracalis is easily detected: extensive bruising and swelling often accompany the tear, the gracalis may well appear dropped, and swelling may even develop around the hock and hind paw.

The dog is likely to be fairly lame and may well have some trouble getting on and off the

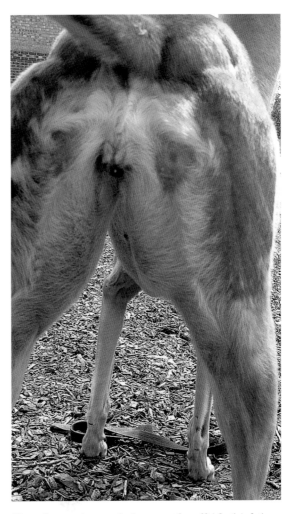

Note the tearing and shape to the offside (right) gracalis. Bad injuries such as this are often difficult to resolve, and the risk of the injury recurring is very high. A long lay-off and plenty of therapy are advised to give the dog the optimum chance of recovery.

bed. It is common practice to ice pack or cold hose the injured gracalis as soon as possible, and this treatment should be repeated at regular intervals over the following forty-eight hours to minimize the internal bleeding and swelling to give the muscle an optimum chance of recovery.

The bruising and swelling may take a while to subside before you can get a really good feel of the damaged tissue. The torn muscle will feel rather like a band of thickened tissue and could be as long as 5–8cm (2–3in). When serious tears like this occur there is usually a lasting visual difference in the shape of the muscle: it will often feel tight and will lose some of its range of motion, which inevitably will affect the dog's performance.

In some cases it may be possible to be stitch the muscle, so with high grade damage it is a good idea to present the dog to a veterinarian who can give you advice on the best course of action. Some of the tears to the gracalis are not this serious; when examining the dog it will depend on the time frame of the injury as to how the muscle will feel. In its earliest stage it will feel soft and doughy around the damage, but you should be able to feel the damaged tissue. There may be some minor swelling and bruising, but over the next few days this should start to disperse and the injury should begin to fibre up and become easier to detect. Over the next week or two it will have settled down, and the scarred and thickened tissue should be easy to feel.

It should be appreciated that damage to the gracalis has a nasty habit of recurring, even in the less pronounced tears; therefore to give the dog the best chance of returning to racing, plenty of attention should be given to the injury and any primary injuries that the dog may have sustained.

Minor tearing around the origin or top of the muscle should be ruled out when examining the gracalis. These tears are often quite small, maybe only 2–3mm in length, though they can sometimes be larger than this, and

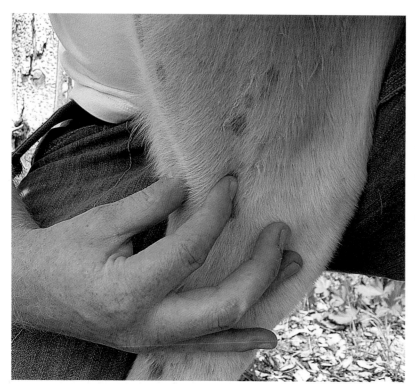

A thickening at the tendonous attachment of the gracalis is a problem that can easily go unnoticed; this is usually the result of a pull or strain. By gently comparing both the tendons it will make it easier to identify a problem.

they will often have had a negative effect on the dog's performance. If it has been carrying such an injury for a long period of time the hind leg will often be obviously wasted as the dog has taken its weight off the injury.

The tendonous attachment at the base of the gracalis is also an important area to check: as you feel down the edges of the muscle and work your way down, you should be able to tell where it becomes tendonous. This tendon at the base of the gracalis has a tendency to become pulled; when feeling both tendons together the damaged one will have a thickened feel to it. This thickening can be quite minimal; only by comparing both the gracalis tendons together will you be able to feel the difference.

While the injured tendon can be easily missed, its effect on the dog's performance won't be, because a dog carrying this sort of injury is likely to be running well below its form.

The Calf Muscle and the Achilles Tendon

The calf is made up of two muscles: the gastrocnemius and the flexor digitorum superficialis, both arising from the femur, and these two muscles then descend into a tendonous attachment known as the Achilles tendon. The flexor digitorum superficialis is almost completely covered by the gastrocnemius; they are both fused together into what would feel like one solid muscle. Both these muscles play a part in the extension of the hock and the flexion of the stifle joint; however, the flexor digitorum superficialis also helps in the flexion of the toes of the hind paw.

The calcanean tendon, more commonly known as the Achilles tendon, is made up of three separate tendons; the main structure is that of the gastrocnemius tendon, but the Achilles also consists of the flexor digitorum superficialis tendon and the combined tendons from the biceps femoris, the semitendinosus and the gracalis. The flexor digitorum superficialis tendon is unlike the other two tendons, in that instead of attaching to the calcaneal tuber, it runs over the heel and divides into four separate tendons, each attaching to the middle toe bone.

Any serious tearing of the Achilles or the calf may have a similar look and feel about it: swelling and thickening down the length of the tendon is not unusual, and on occasions the whole of the hock area may be swollen. This swelling will probably make the location of the damage difficult to pinpoint, and caution must be taken as swelling works in a downward direction and may well be caused by an injury further up the leg. Although this may seem obvious, if a proper examination of the dog is not undertaken then injuries like this can easily be misdiagnosed. The most common of these is damage to the gracalis, where extensive bruising and swelling often make their way down the leg and sit around the hock and Achilles region; in extreme cases the swelling may even reach the toes.

Over the next few days the swelling should start to subside and you should be able to feel the location of any tear that has occurred in the

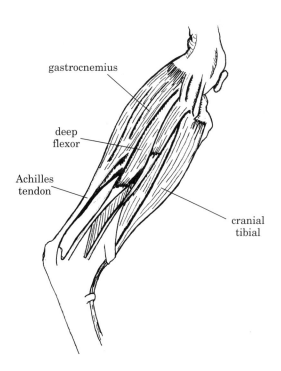

The Achilles tendon and the calf muscles.

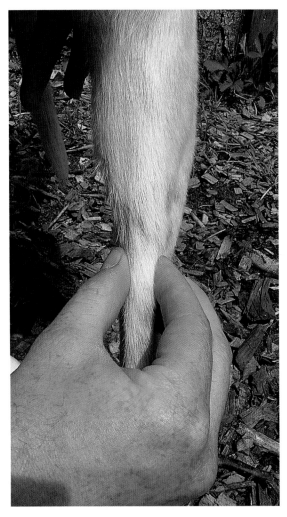

By gently feeling along the length of the Achilles tendon and around the calf muscle you should be able to feel any tearing or swelling. It is important to gently feel both Achilles tendons simultaneously, as a minor thickening of one of the tendons could easily be missed.

calf or tendon. These tears most commonly feel like a small knot or pea, and can be felt easily when the muscle and tendon is rolled between finger and thumb. These tears may well occur anywhere in the calf or along the length of the tendon, or at the attachment to the heel, which is also the point where the flexor tendon passes over the heel. Differentiating between which tendon or tendons have been torn or damaged

is difficult, and it is not until the veterinarian opens up the leg that the true nature of the damage can be assessed.

Even though tears to the Achilles tendon are quite serious, if the dog is given a long layoff and a high level of care and attention, the prognosis for racing is still fairly good. Tearing up in the calf muscle is not as serious as tearing in the Achilles, though again, caution must be taken as to the seriousness of the damage.

When inspecting and feeling the calf muscle it is good practice to check the size and shape of the muscle, since any wasting or deterioration has probably been caused by an injury further up the leg. There is a good chance that the gracalis and thigh will also look smaller or thinner, as the dog is probably compensating for the damage and underusing the leg. Any damage to the hip, the TFL, the groin, the whip or the gracalis should be ruled out. However, the wasting may just be damage to the calf itself. Each avenue should be investigated to help you obtain a good picture of the dog's physical health.

Hock Injuries

Injuries to the hock are seen at many different levels, but it must be recognized that the offside hock is especially prone to damage in the track dog. As the greyhound turns anti-clockwise it is the offside hind leg that generates the power to push the dog around the bend. This increased pressure makes the offside hind leg, and especially the hock joint, vulnerable to damage.

The broken or fractured hock is by far the most common break or fracture that the greyhound sustains through racing. A dislocation of the hock, which is caused by a tear to a ligament or ligaments that support the tarsal bones, is also another serious injury that occurs to the hock. While these injuries will undoubtedly cause the dog to break down during racing or at least be very lame after the run, it is highly unlikely that an injury such as this will not be picked up on a race night.

The veterinarian at the track should be able to stabilize the hock until the dog can be more thoroughly checked with X-rays to establish the extent of the damage.

The location and the severity of the damage will largely dictate if the dog has anything left of its racing career. With injuries such as this you must have total confidence in your veterinarian, and not all vets are experienced when it comes to racing injuries; it is therefore imperative that you take the greatest care in your selection of a veterinarian. Furthermore, the rehabilitation of the injury can be just as important as the surgical repair, and this is when it is essential to have the advice of a good vet in order to give the dog the optimum chance of recovery.

Very small chips or cracks can be found on the tarsal bones, or indeed anywhere around the hock. These minor injuries can usually be detected as small lumps on the bone, which you should be able to feel by gently rolling your thumb around the tarsal bones. This type of small chip or crack can often make the dog quite lame, but due to the intricacy of the damage they may be difficult to detect, and can be easily misdiagnosed.

Like many serious injuries, the cost to put the dog right can far outweigh the cost of the dog itself, and for the owner or trainer any serious injury can be a gamble. While plenty of dogs come back from a broken hock as good as they were before, there are plenty that have had a marked loss in performance, struggled to make the grade, or just suffer from soreness after a run.

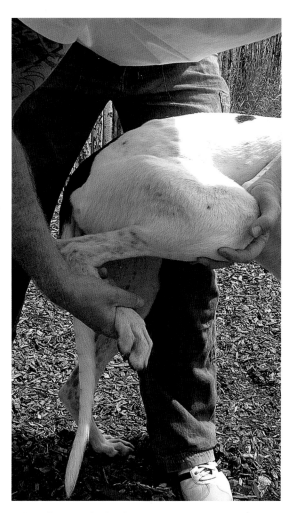

When flexing the hock it is important to note the distance between hock and paw to observe the range of motion. This is just as important as trying to uncover any pain or discomfort in the joint.

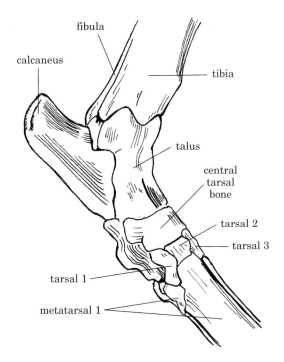

The bones of the hock joint.

As well as suffering fracture or dislocation, the hock has a tendency to strain or sprain in varying degrees. Sometimes these injuries can be minimal, but if the dog isn't examined between each run they are easily missed – and if they are, and the dog carries on running, in all likelihood the injury will badly deteriorate. When checking the hock, mild pain will probably be evident on flexion, and there may even be a slight swelling around the front of the hock.

If the sprain is more serious the dog will probably be walking lame, or taking weight off the injured leg when it is standing. Pain will be evident on flexion, and a minor swelling will probably be detectable around the hock. Learning to feel the hock in its healthy state will greatly help you to detect any swelling, however minor, and also to feel any small lumps or bumps that shouldn't be there. Gently rolling the hock between your fingers and thumb will help you get a good feel for the bone, while gently stroking the hock with your fingertips will help you feel any slight swelling over the bone. It is of benefit to squat behind the dog and compare both hocks together as this will give you a better chance of feeling any differences in the structure.

Like the wrist, any detection of lumps, bumps, swelling or general pain in the hock should be treated with the utmost circumspection, and it is wise to have the dog examined by a veterinarian, and to have X-rays taken in order to rule out any bone damage.

In this chapter I have discussed some of the most common problems that the greyhound sustains. Beyond this lie many other injuries, such as pectineus (groin), the sartorius (whip muscle), biceps femoris (thigh), deep pectoral (chest) and crania tibial (shin). What is important is that the handler uses his knowledge to look and feel over the whole of the dog, and to check for any injuries or problems. Each and every muscle, tendon, ligament and bone can become damaged, so it is important to check the whole dog. For the novice handler or trainer it is important to call a veterinarian for advice and assistance when an injury is detected.

CHAPTER TEN

Foot Problems

The feet or paws of the greyhound are crucial, and any injury or problem that is left untreated or even unnoticed could have serious repercussions. It is important that the handler washes and examines the feet on a daily basis to rule out any such problems. Start off by washing the paws in warm, soapy water, and then cleaning the nails and nail beds with a nailbrush to remove any dirt or sand; take particular care around any sore nail beds.

The feet should then be examined for problems such as infected toes, bruised or cracked nails, torn ligaments, broken toes, corns or warts, split webs or sand burns. It is important that a novice handler can recognize these problems, and has a basic idea of how to treat them.

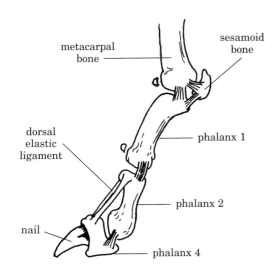

The toe joint.

NAIL INJURIES

Infected Nails

Infected nail beds are often caused by dirt getting into the bed and around the top of the toe. If the dirt is not cleaned away, then a hard crust may form and this makes it easy for fungi to invade the tissue around the nail bed. Cuts and broken skin can also leave the toe susceptible to infection. Infected nails usually look red and sore around the bed; in the worst cases there may be swelling with the skin receding. In some circumstances there may even be pus evident, and the hair will have disappeared or receded from the toe end.

It is important to treat these conditions before the dog is returned to the track.

The area should be cleaned with warm soapy water with a splash of Dettol – it is important to clear out all the dirt – and it can then be treated with antiseptic spray or ointment. It is essential to try and keep the nail bed clean and dry to help the problem heal up; it may be beneficial to strap up the foot for a couple of days, and keep a rubber glove over the strapping to keep it dry.

Bruised and Cracked Nails

Signs of bruising include blood within the nail, and the dog is often lame because the nail is painful due to the pressure within it. The nail should be clipped or filed shorter to reduce the pressure on it, and it should be inspected daily to rule out any infection.

A split or cracked nail should be washed, cleaned and then trimmed back to reduce the pressure on it. The nail should be sprayed with an antiseptic spray, and then coated with a nail mender to glue it up. If the nail is split or cracked badly it may be necessary to clip it right back above the damage, and if it has to be clipped back high up it is likely to bleed a lot. To stop the bleeding, make up a solution of one part hydrogen peroxide and ten parts water, soak a blob of cotton wool in the solution, and apply it firmly to the nail. The nail should then be bandaged up for several days while it begins to heal. The dressing should be changed daily and the nail cleansed. Leaving the nail open invites infection into the nail bed.

PAD INJURIES

Split Webs
Split webs can vary in their seriousness, and can be anything from a small cut at the end of the web to a full web split. Any sort of tearing of the flesh will usually need the whole web splitting back; moreover, partial tears will often open up each time the dog runs, so surgical repair is often the answer.

Sand Burns
It is important to check the skin between the pads on the underside of the foot for any sand burns or cuts. Small cuts and burns need to be cleaned and treated to avoid infection; any serious cuts and tearing of the tissue will cause a much bigger problem because deep cuts are prone to reopening even if the tissue is stitched up and the dog is given a long rest. The problem is often caused by the flexor tendons being weak, so the toes overspread, allowing the foot to have contact with the sand; therefore as well as treating the cut, it is a good idea to try and strengthen the flexor tendons with plenty of physical massage.

It is advisable to give the dog a minimum of two months' rest if the cut is bad. When you return the dog to galloping, you can tape the toes up to stop them spreading; however, when it returns to the track, the rules of racing will not permit it to run with any sort of support bandage.

If the cut reopens it is unlikely that the foot will repair; I have seen dogs stitched up and treated several times, but the outcome is often the same. The old-fashioned method is to fill the cut, and between the pads, with Stockholm tar (a sticky black substance obtainable from a chemist): when the dog runs, the tar protects the cut and keeps out any sand or dirt. While this is not ideal for the dog, you may find it is the only option other than retirement.

Cracked Pads
Dry and cracked pads can be a real problem, especially if they are really sore; the best way to treat the problem is to mix potassium permanganate and water in a bucket and soak the dog's feet in it. When mixing the solution I don't use an exact measure, but put a good two or three tablespoons into a half bucket of water and then add more potassium if needed. When the dog's feet have been soaked in the solution the feet will stain purple – don't be alarmed, this is normal.

Soak the feet in the mixture for ten minutes twice a day for as long as treatment is needed; in some cases where a dog has very bad feet this may well be an on-going procedure.

Corns
Corns can be a real problem in the greyhound. A dog that is walking very lame but with no obvious sign of injury will often be suffering from a corn or corns.

A corn is like a growth on the pad that grows inwards due to the pressure of the dog's pad walking on a hard surface, and will be very painful when pressure is applied to the pad. It is usually the size of a matchstick head, and has a smooth surface on the rough pad; sometimes it may have a slight discoloration, or look almost white on the pad. I use three different treatments for corns:

• A kitchen spray containing bleach sprayed

on to the corn can kill the virus or growth. Treatment once a day for several days will sometimes rectify the problem.

- The toe could have a poultice applied to draw out the corn; when the pad is softened and the corn looks ready to come out, it can be squeezed out with your fingers.
- Surgical removal of the corn; in serious cases the pad and last digit may be removed to spare the dog any further suffering.

TOE INJURIES

Broken Toes

Broken toes and torn ligaments are injuries that show very similar symptoms, namely pain, inflammation, swelling and heat. Only an X-ray will show the full picture, when breaks, chips or dislocation should be evident.

The collateral ligaments control the sideways movement of the toe, and if the ligament becomes pulled or sprained then a soft, painful swelling will be evident around the joint. Cold-water therapy should be applied for at least the first forty-eight hours, and then a spirit blister can be used to strengthen the toe.

A dislocated toe involves a complete tear of the collateral ligament; the toe will have a sideways displacement and will be painful for the first few days. This type of injury needs the assistance of a veterinarian, as surgery may be the best course of action.

an example of how the joint loses stability

A severed ligament of the toe joint. The lack of support causes a sideways displacement of the toe.

Thickened Toe

The thickened toe is caused by injury to the joint capsule of the toe joint. The joint fluid often leaks out and turns to fibrous tissue, causing a hard thickening around the joint. This is known as a thick toe.

When the toe is first diagnosed, cold water therapy should be applied for forty-eight hours, then a hot kaolin poultice applied to the toe every eight hours until the swelling subsides. The kaolin should be heated up in its pot by boiling it in a pan of water; before applying it to the injured toe it should be tested with the elbow to make sure it is not too hot. It should be applied liberally to the toe, which should then be strapped up.

It can be beneficial to have the nail removed or cut back to take the pressure off the toe; in this case veterinary advice should be sought by the handler, particularly the novice.

After about a fortnight the toe should have settled down, and some massage and toe movement can begin; this should be done to reduce any fibrous or scarred tissue. Use your finger and thumb to massage and work the injured toe; this should be done quite vigorously for a few minutes to break down the scarred tissue. Then cold hose the toe for a few minutes; repeat just the cold-hose therapy three or four times a day for the next three days. It is important that the toe is massaged three or four days apart so that the cold-water therapy can remove the dead tissue.

I prefer to try and save the toe before contemplating surgery to have it removed, or even a part of it. If a dog loses a toe it can have a dramatic effect on its performance because it will struggle to balance properly.

Spike Injuries

Spikes in the toes are not uncommon due to the nature of the sport; they are usually observed as a small puncture in the toe or webbing. The wound should be kept clean and treated with antiseptic spray, cream or wound powder; spike injuries are susceptible to infection so it is good practice to clean and treat them.

DEEP AND SUPERFICIAL FLEXOR TENDON INJURIES

The flexor tendons originate as muscles that run down the back of the foreleg; the muscle turns tendonous above the wrist, and then runs inside the accessory carpal bone before separating into five tendons. The deep and the superficial flexor muscles and tendons are totally independent, and each performs its own task. The superficial tendon attaches to the P2 bone, while the deep tendon attaches to the P3 bone; their role is to counteract the pull of the extensor tendons that run down the front of the toes.

Pulls and strains to these tendons are not uncommon, and can be detected as a soft thickening of the tendon; this injury usually occurs to tendon five in the nearside paw and tendon two in the offside paw. While in some cases the tendon can become quite angry and swollen and cause the dog lameness, it must also be noted that less pronounced thickenings

can occur to these tendons, and these can easily be missed. To get a better feel of the tendons you can extend the toes so that the tendons become tight; any minor swelling can then be felt by gently stroking the tendons with your finger or thumb. As the damage starts to heal and the swelling subsides, the tendon will stay thick but it will become much harder and fibrous.

Damage to these tendons is nearly always classed as a secondary injury and is often the result of soreness around the c-t junction and the trapezius; it is therefore important to correct this damage in order to stop any recurring problems to the tendon.

Problems to the flexor tendons of the hind limb are far less frequent but must still be checked for when examining the hind paws.

Surgical removal of the tendon is an option, but it is one I use as a last resort. Cross-friction massage, and detection and treatment of the accompanying primary injury, will often see a reduction in the size of the tendon, and

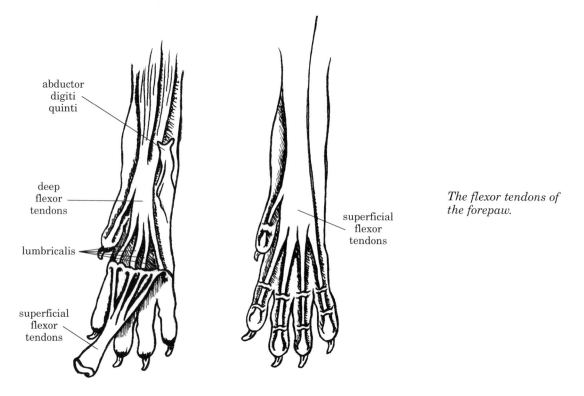

abductor
digiti
quinti

deep
flexor
tendons

lumbricalis

superficial
flexor
tendons

superficial
flexor
tendons

The flexor tendons of the forepaw.

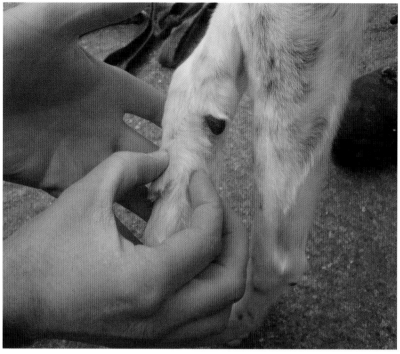

Thickening to the flexor tendons is not uncommon; however, even in formerly ruptured tendons it is important to check them after each run to rule out any fresh pain or swelling of the tendon. It must also be noted that a high proportion of these injuries are the result of a problem in and around the c-t junction.

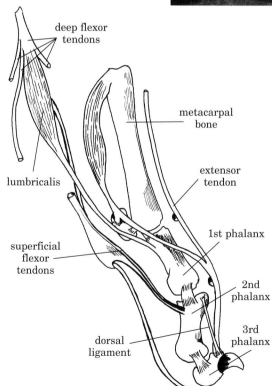

Toe joints and connective ligaments and tendons.

will reduce the chance of the injury recurring. Tendons that are not treated, especially when the primary injury is not detected, will often recur and cause the dog further problems.

When a dog is walking lame it is vitally important to examine the paws thoroughly. It may have suffered small cuts to the pads or have developed corns or warts, minute foreign objects can get lodged in the pads, nail beds can become sore and infected, or the nails may become cracked.

When a dog is walking very lame for more than a couple of days it is very unlikely that the problem is a muscular injury, but is more likely to be a bone, ligament or foot problem.

CHAPTER ELEVEN

Injury Rehabilitation and Massage

It is important to understand that the prevention of injuries is much better than cure. Learning how to detect injuries and getting them treated at an early stage will definitely help reduce the number of serious injuries that your greyhounds sustain. However, as a trainer you are going to have to deal with all different types of injury, and it is important that you know some of the basics. I will explain some of the best techniques that I have used over the years.

TREATING MUSCLE DAMAGE

Any serious injury to the muscle or tendon will undoubtedly be spotted at the track by you or the veterinarian. When an injury like this is seen, it is important to treat it with cold-water or ice-pack therapy as soon as possible. All tracks have at least a cold-water tap that you can use to run over the affected limb. After a further inspection of the damage the dog can be put away.

Before loading the dog on the transport at the end of the night it is good practice to hose off the injured leg again with cold water for a good five minutes; then when you return to your own kennels you can repeat the process again. Some may consider this to be a pointless and time-wasting exercise, but on the contrary, it is extremely beneficial to the injury. Cold-water therapy is very important because it helps reduce the inflammation and it removes waste products from the damaged area. This can be very important in how the injury will heal in the long term.

The following morning you can take a good look at the damage to assess how bad it is. Over the next forty-eight to seventy-two hours the bruising and bleeding may spread and the inflammation increase, and it is over this period that you should cold hose the injured area for five to ten minutes at least four or five times a day. I personally prefer to use a cold hosepipe rather than an ice pack because of the damage you can do to the muscle tissues if you leave the ice pack on for too long.

The day after the injury, and depending on its location and severity, the dog should be taken to the veterinarian for a second opinion and advice as to treatment. There is often a window of opportunity that should not be missed if the dog is in need of a surgical repair. Injuries to the TFL and the gracalis often repair very well with surgery, so it is important that the greyhound is inspected by the vet as early as possible.

Recovery from Injury

Again, how long the dog will need to recover will largely depend on the severity of the injury. As a rule you should confine it to a small concrete paddock, or keep it on a lead for a minimum of three weeks. If the injury is severe and warrants further time to heal, then the handler must use his own initiative and give the dog as long as it needs; any strain or stress on the tear could well cause more damage if the dog were allowed to run free in a large run or paddock.

During the initial three-week period put the dog in a magnetic field therapy box if you have one, set on a low frequency, to reduce the inflammation and calm the injury down. When the injury has settled down at around two to three weeks, gentle exercise such as walking can begin; this should be gradually built up over the coming weeks.

A programme of massage and stretching of the injured limb can be started. Note that it is important to massage the limb thoroughly before you start any flexion and extension; this should be done very gently to begin with, and then built up over the course of time. If you have not been advised on this practice, then it is beneficial to get veterinary advice.

After around five to eight weeks (depending on the injury and its severity) the dog can start to run free or begin galloping. Again, this needs to be introduced sensibly. It is no good giving it a full-on 600m gallop when it has been convalescing for several weeks: the work should be built up gradually over a period of time.

How many gallops a dog should be given before returning it to the track would depend on the injury; a minimum of three or four gallops is beneficial to try and build up the strength of the injury. These gallops will help increase the dog's fitness and also apply some much needed pressure to the injury; if it cannot stand up to a short gallop, there is a risk that it could break down completely if it is taken back to a race track.

TREATING LIGAMENT DAMAGE

Damage to the ligament and joints can be seen in various levels of severity. The wrist, the hock and the toes are the most commonly injured joints, but damage to the shoulder and knee joints occurs from time to time. In my experience injuries to the elbow and hip joints are rare.

Injury to the Wrist
Like the muscle injury, you should apply cold-water therapy immediately after the race and, like the muscle, at regular intervals afterwards. When checking the wrist the following day it is important to try and determine the amount of pain there is, how much swelling is around the front of the wrist, and more importantly if there is any swelling around the base of the stopper bone.

If there is swelling of any degree you should take the dog for an X-ray to rule out any bone damage. If there is bone damage, then depending on the injury, the vet will decide the best course of treatment. If there is no bone damage the vet will probably inject the wrist to help reduce any inflammation and to stabilize it. It is important to continue cold-water therapy for the first seventy-two hours, and then possibly apply a spirit blister to try and heal the wrist (the veterinarian should prescribe the best form of treatment).

The dog should be confined to a small paddock or to lead work for at least a month, and then gradually brought back to fitness. If you are lucky enough to be training near the sea it can be of great benefit to the injury to gallop a dog with a wrist injury at the beach; you can take it into the sea for a good five minutes before the gallop, and then again afterwards. Sea water seems to have great healing properties: never underestimate the power of nature.

A programme of extension, flexion and rotation of the wrist should be started from day one of the injury, providing there is no bone damage. Gently extending and flexing the wrist even at an early stage will help remove any waste products, and prevent the joint stiffening up. The wrist can be flexed and extended halfway through the cold-water therapy, which should be undertaken three or four times a day in the initial few days. Be aware that if you blister the wrist you may have to interrupt any such therapy while the blister treatment settles down.

Any dog in my care that has a wrist injury would be given flexion and extension exercises on a daily basis in conjunction with massage to the joint. This simple exercise can make a great deal of difference to the health of the wrist joint, and is one that any trainer can easily learn to do. It is simply a case of extending and flexing the wrist back and forth through its range of motion, then rotating it in a circular motion clockwise, and then anti-clockwise.

In the initial stages the movement should be gentle as the injury is likely to be sore and painful, but as healing progresses the treatment can become much faster and firmer.

Injury to the Stopper Bone

Ligament sprains of the stopper bone are critical, so it is important that they get some form of therapy. Spraining of the attachments to the stopper can be serious, even if the sprain is mild. I have seen a lot of dogs retired because of this injury: as soon as the dog is given any serious work the injury will flare up again, and it will be lame. Again, cold-water therapy is a must, as soon and as regularly as possible, and an X-ray of the bone should be taken to rule out bone damage. The vet will prescribe the best course of action, which may well mean injecting the wrist and the use of a spirit blister.

After treatment, a routine of moving the stopper bone should be started. Standing over the dog and facing backwards, flex the wrist to halfway; this should loosen off the stopper bone so you can get some sideways movement and some vertical movement. Ten times each way would be sufficient, then massage the stopper bone with liniment and repeat the process.

Sprains and strains to the stopper should not be taken lightly. A long lay-off is important, with a minimum of three months' rest even if the injury is mild.

Injury to the Hock

Ligament damage to the hock is very similar to that of the wrist. The joint will often appear swollen, and will be painful on flexion. Any breaks or chips to the multiple bones of the hock need to be ruled out before treatment begins, so veterinary assistance should be sought.

If there is no bone damage, then like the wrist, the hock should be given cold-water therapy for several days to help reduce any swelling. Gentle flexion and extension exercises can be started to keep the joint from seizing up, and also to help flush out any waste products. Like the wrist, the use of magnetic field therapy treatment on a low setting can greatly aid the recovery of the joint.

Diet for the Injured Dog

When a dog is injured some trainers like to change its food to a basic or resting diet. However, while it doesn't need to be fed such a high protein or quality protein diet, it is still important that it receives the right nutrients to assist healing. During injury rehabilitation it is good practice to supply the injured dog with a multi-vitamin or a fish supplement.

TREATMENT MACHINES IN INJURY REHABILITATION

Over the years I have had experience of many of the various machines that can be used in the rehabilitation of injuries. There are several types of machine that work in different ways to help in the healing of injuries, including magnetic field therapy, ultrasound, TENS, laser and infrared therapy. It is important that as a handler you obtain veterinary permission and advice about the correct methods of using any therapeutic machines.

The Magnetic Field Therapy Unit

I would recommend that the novice starts off with a machine such as the magnetic field therapy unit. These come in different variations, such as a complete box that the dog sits in, a flat square board that can be placed in the car or under the dog's bed, and a unit with individual pads that are placed on the injured limbs.

The problem when using the machine with pads is that the dog must be held while receiving treatment, and this can be very time-consuming; however, when using the box the dog is placed into a cage-type unit, so the handler can be getting on with other chores while the dog is receiving treatment.

Magnetic field therapy works by sending electromagnetic pulses through the dog's body, which affect the blood vessels and the flow of blood within the tissues. On a low frequency blood vessels tighten up and become narrower, restricting the flow of blood, so in effect you have a situation similar to that of a cold hose or an ice pack. This can be very effective when dealing with muscle tears or in reducing swelling.

On a high frequency the effect is directly the opposite, in that the blood vessels dilate thereby allowing more blood, and therefore more oxygen, into the muscles. This is also very good for removing muscle waste, and at the same time it can help to relieve pain. What is important is that as the dead cells and debris are removed, indirectly this helps to rejuvenate and rebuild new, healthy cells. In effect it therefore not only speeds up the healing process, but promotes better, in the sense of stronger, healing.

For the novice handler, a magnetic field therapy box is definitely the best machine to start with. When the greyhound is in the box the whole of the dog is being treated, which means that in effect any minor injury that has been missed will still get treatment. This is important if you feel that you may not be detecting some of the more minor injuries. In contrast to this, ultrasound and laser therapy machines only directly treat one injury at a time.

I personally find the box to be an important asset to any handler, particularly for dogs with serious injuries such as breaks or bad tears; these respond much better when assisted with magnetic field therapy.

In my opinion there is also substantial benefit in using the magnetic field therapy unit on older dogs that frequently come back sore or stiff after a race; I will often leave an older dog in the box overnight following a hard race to help it recover.

It is important to note that back injuries also respond very well to magnetic field therapy. Soreness or tightness, especially around the c-t junction, will heal or recover much faster.

The magnetic field therapy box can also be used as a race-day tone up: twenty minutes on full power is similar to giving the dog a morning gallop, but without the risk of sustaining injury. A degree of caution is advised, however, as some dogs that are left in the box for a long time on a race day will not perform very well; it must be noted that each dog seems to react differently to being left in the box, and while one may benefit, another may run badly.

The Ultrasound Machine

The ultrasound uses ultrasonic waves to thermally increase the blood flow into the damaged tissue. A lubricant or gel is applied to the area to be treated to create a contact between machine and dog, and this should not be interrupted during the treatment.

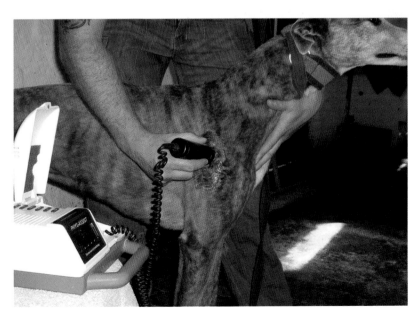

The ultrasound is a valuable tool in the treatment of racing injuries. However, it is important that the handler has some knowledge of, or training on a machine such as this before he starts treating his dogs. Untold damage can be inflicted on your dogs if you misuse a machine such as this.

The ultrasound is exceptionally good at treating tears to the muscle or muscle sheath, and also thickened tendons. Ultrasounds are normally used at a rate of one treatment a day for five days, and in this time you can often feel the difference in the tissue. Holes, tears and a thickening of tissue usually diminish in size even after the first five days of treatment.

Depending on the injury, more than one set of treatment with the ultrasound can often be given, such as five days of treatment and then a week off, followed by another five-day course.

It is important that you do not overuse the ultrasound, and that you follow the manufacturer's guidelines that accompany the machine or those advised by your veterinarian. Overuse of the ultrasound or incorrect use can lead to serious burns and damage to muscle tissue, and can weaken small bones. I prefer not to use the ultrasound on any bony area such as the wrist or hock.

The TENS Machine

The TENS machine can also be used by the handler. Two electrodes pass an electric current through the muscle, with the effect of both relaxing and contracting it.

The TENS machine is often used for toning or building up withered muscles; I most commonly use it to relieve lower back pain and hip problems. A greyhound that constantly misses the break or shows a slower than normal acceleration to the first turn is quite often suffering from lower back or hip problems, and by treating these areas over a two-week period you will often see a marked improvement in its performance. I would generally treat a dog twice a day for four days, then two days off, repeating this cycle until I felt it was sound.

When using the TENS it is important to use a gel to get a good connection; it is also important that you increase the output of the machine gradually, starting it on a low level and then building it up to a level that the dog can stand. I have used the TENS machine on myself so am well aware of its capabilities; I suffer from sciatica and lower back pain, and this machine works wonders!

The TENS machine can also be used as an injury detection tool; the pen can be used to run over the muscles to help locate areas of pain. Where there is inflammation within the muscles then that muscle acts as a conductor, which enhances the sensitivity of an injury. Injuries

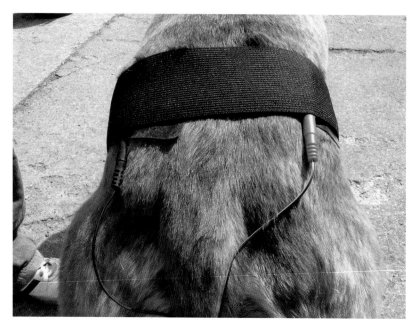

The TENS machine is very effective at treating hip and lower back pain. Like the ultrasound, it is important that the handler has some experience of using the machine before he starts treating his dogs.

The pen that often comes with various TENS or nerve stimulators can be used effectively at diagnosing muscle problems. It can often pick up soreness or pain in a muscle that is sometimes missed under physical examination.

that are difficult to detect, such as in the hips or the back, can be identified more easily when the muscle is scrutinized under the pen. Again, it is important that the handler seeks advice from a veterinarian before using this equipment.

The Hydrotherapy Bath

The hydrotherapy bath or jacuzzi can be used to treat several problems in the greyhound. It is a small bath where water jets apply pressure to the dog's body, and will help to treat muscle soreness, to reduce inflammation to areas of bruising or sprains, and to disperse fluids that are produced from any sort of muscle damage. It can be used to help improve muscle tone in dogs that have been laid off or rested for a lengthy period, and is a very useful therapy for dogs that have endured a strenuous workout, or that are in competition or coursing events on successive days, as it helps the body recover from any minor aches and pains.

The dog should be placed in the bath for no longer than ten minutes, although five is usually sufficient. The water temperature should always be checked to prevent any skin damage.

The hydro bath can also be used to freshen up a dog on a race day. A quick bath on the morning of a race can do wonders for a dog, though it is important not to overdo it – a couple of minutes is sufficient.

A greyhound enjoys a relaxing bath after a hard day in the slips.

127

THE SKILL OF MASSAGE

Massage is a vital part of conditioning and race preparation, and an important part of injury rehabilitation. It involves a procedure of rubbing, stroking, kneading and stretching motions, and to massage a dog correctly should take a minimum of ten minutes.

There are several benefits to be gained from massage, including an increase of blood flow to the muscle, the breakdown of fibrous and scarred tissue, improved muscle tone, and the build-up of withered or wasted muscles. A greyhound that is in training should be massaged at least once a day, and it is important that they are massaged both before and after any serious workout. Furthermore, I would massage a dog three times in a day during the conditioning phase of its training programme (the point in a cycle where the greyhound is approaching peak fitness).

Some handlers are under the impression that a race-day massage can improve a dog's performance by several lengths, however I would contest this assumption. While it is quite plausible that with a good nutrition, exercise and massage programme it is possible to find a few racing lengths over a short period of time, it is impossible to find any great improvement with just one massage on a race day. A greyhound in training should be massaged on a continuing daily basis if it is to receive any true benefits from massage.

The use of a liniment or embrocation when massaging is also important because these help with blood circulation and also disperse any waste products that are left after a vigorous workout. Liniments also have healing properties that assist the recovery of minor muscle, tendon and joint damage. To apply these it is easier and less wasteful if you pour the liniment into a regular spray bottle (if you are using a spray bottle that has contained a liquid previously, such as kitchen or bathroom cleaner, be sure to clean the bottle out thoroughly).

When applying the liniment to the greyhound it is best to spray each muscle group in turn, working it into the coat immediately. For instance, apply the liniment to the shoulder muscles, and then massage it in. Liniments are often highly volatile and need to be worked in immediately, so if you apply the liniment to the whole of the dog and then massage it in, you will probably have lost the potency of the liniment by the time you finish the dog.

General Massage

Start off by straddling the greyhound and working the whole neck area in a smooth, circular rubbing motion. Then move to the shoulders and start again in a circular motion, before using your fingers to work more specifically along the line and contours that separate the muscles. It is important not to miss the front of the shoulder and chest area.

Then work up and down the foreleg in a long, smooth rubbing motion with the palms of your hands cupped around the legs; make sure you work the length of the leg and the carpal tendon.

Lift the wrist off the ground and let it hang down, and with a cupped hand gently rub and roll the palm of your hand around the wrist in a circular movement; use your finger and thumbs to rub the metacarpals and surrounding tendons.

Moving on to the lower chest and the rib area, start with your hands under the armpits and then work back and upwards towards the dog's loins in long strokes. Repeat this several times to work the chest and abdominal muscles.

Starting on the back, place your hands on either side of the spine and in a short to-and-fro movement work your way all along the dog's back. Use your fingers and knuckles to knead and massage gently into the deeper muscles.

Then place your hands on the dog's back and with your palms facing outwards, pull your hands downwards towards the ribs. What this is doing is working across the true flow of the muscle, which helps stretch out any tightness or mild muscle spasm within the back muscles.

When working the hind limbs I prefer to stand directly behind the dog; some handlers like to straddle the dog and face backwards.

Work in large and small circular motions, starting on the hips and working down the legs, covering all of the musculature. It is important to come below the stifle and work along the front of the shin and around the calf muscle.

Like the wrist, it is also important not to miss the hock and the metatarsals; again, use your palms and fingers to work around the area.

After working the whole dog it can be beneficial to massage the muscles with a little more accuracy. Standing to the dog's near side, bend over it and use both hands in a left-right, left-right motion to massage each muscle group.

I would start with the offside shoulder and work the chest and ribcage before moving on to the hind legs. It is important to rotate the hands quickly, at the same time keeping them moving with the lie of the coat – don't work against it. Then move round to the nearside and repeat the process on the offside of the greyhound.

When you have finished, lubricate your hands with a little olive oil or sunflower oil and friction massage the whole of the dog for a good few minutes more. Then take a large towel and give the dog another massage with it, finishing off by sweeping it down the length of the back a few times over.

Cross-Friction Massage

Cross-friction massage is a technique I learned many years ago, and can be used to greatly assist certain tendon injuries. The flexor tendon runs down the back of the metacarpals, and a ruptured flexor is a fairly common injury that can benefit from this type of massage.

When the tendon has healed it will often be thickened with a lot of scarred tissue, and it is this scarred or dead tissue that needs to be removed to help prevent the injury recurring.

Start off by working your thumb back and forth across the thickened tendon; it needs to be worked in quite an aggressive manner in order to aggravate the scarred tissue and break it up. The tendon needs to be worked for a few minutes, which will probably mean you will have to change thumbs, as they can become numb.

After four or five minutes' massage you need to immediately run the tendon under a cold running hosepipe for several minutes to reduce any inflammation and help flush away any dead tissue. The tendon will then need cold-water therapy or icing off (applying an ice pack) three times a day for the next four days. After four or five days the tendon can be massaged again and the process repeated: it is important that the tendon is rested for several days between each massage, and that it is only treated with cold water or ice.

After three or four weeks of treatment the tendon should be seriously reduced in size and should have a much healthier feel to it. The therapy has two great aspects: first, it removes all the scarred tissue and dead cells; and second, it encourages the regeneration of new muscle cells and tissue, which greatly improves the health of the tendon.

Isolation Massage

Massage of a damaged part of the dog's structure is known as isolation massage; this may be a muscle, a tendon or a joint. It can be used to disperse fluid from an injured joint, to stretch a tight muscle, or to improve the circulation to a damaged area.

When trying to remove fluid from a track leg, a wrist or a toe injury, the damage should be stroked with a light pressure in the direction of the dog's coat or hair. A liniment can be sprayed on to the affected area to help remove the inflammation and waste.

Before commencing the massage, cold-water therapy should be applied for forty-eight hours; kaolin poultices can also be used.

PHYSIOTHERAPY

Learning some of the basics of physiotherapy will greatly assist your ability to treat your greyhounds. Some injuries will improve immensely if you take the time each day to give the dog some physiotherapy. One of the most common and career-threatening injuries, the dreaded sprained wrist, can be remarkably improved if a dog has suffered a serious sprain, and can often mean the difference between it being able to keep running and taking an early retirement.

Most of the basic manoeuvres are not difficult to learn and are basically a case of extension, flexion and rotation of the affected or connected joint. When a veterinarian prescribes treatment for an injury he will often give the handler some advice on some of the basic movement techniques.

Physiotherapy of the Joint

The majority of joints in the greyhound are known as synovial joints, where two opposing bones are held in place by a series of fibrous tissues known as ligaments. The end of each bone is encased in a synovial membrane, which is itself a fibrous capsular ligament. This synovial membrane supplies a joint fluid that lubricates the joint so the two bones can glide easily over one another. Synovial fluid is also important because it provides the joint with vital nutrients, and helps remove waste products from the joint.

When trauma occurs to the joint the flow of synovial fluid into the joint can be disrupted and slow right down, and then the ligaments and tendons become dry and lose their flexibility. The bone and cartilage can become brittle, and there may even be bony changes as the bones rub on each other and the joint loses its natural tension. All this aggravation in the joint can cause it to swell, which in turn can cause stretching of the connective ligaments and soft tissue, making the whole area sore and painful and leaving the dog with restricted movement in the joint.

Movement of a sore and painful joint can dramatically affect its ability to recover. Complete rest can have a totally negative effect on the joint because it stiffens up and loses its range of motion, thus complicating the situation. By simply moving the joint back and forth any unwanted fluid can be pumped away, and will also help soften any thickened

tissue that may be causing tightness within the joint.

The degree of movement applied to a joint is crucial and the handler should proceed with care. The recovery process can be greatly assisted by simply working the joint gently back and forth through its range of motion for a few minutes once or twice a day; this amount should be ample. While some strains are mild and will respond to quite aggressive therapy, other more serious strains will need a much gentler approach, to promote healing at a slower pace. It is largely a matter of common sense.

The principal joints that become injured in the greyhound are the wrist and the hock. If there is any major pain or swelling in either of these joints, the dog should be taken for a veterinary examination and possibly an X-ray to rule out a fracture.

Physiotherapy of the Muscle

Physiotherapy of the muscles is similar to that of the joints, and flexing and extending a muscle through its range of motion will promote its health immensely. However, whereas with a joint you can start movement pretty much from day one, with a muscle it is important not to start pulling and stretching for at least two to three weeks, depending on the injury.

With a torn shoulder, for example, you would start by massaging the muscle to warm and tone it up. Then stand over the dog and hold the forearm just below the elbow, and raise the elbow upwards and then back down and forwards to extend the shoulder. This movement should start off quite gently, and over the course of two or three weeks would become progressively stronger.

The purpose of movement therapy is to prevent fibrous or damaged tissue from restricting the range of movement in the joint. If there is excessive fibrous tissue binding the tear, then the tear becomes weaker, and when subjected to extreme pressure the chance of the damage recurring is much greater.

CHAPTER TWELVE

The Older Greyhound

THE VETERAN RACER

Some trainers consider that once a greyhound is past four years of age it is 'over the hill', or well past its 'sell by' date. Older dogs are often moved on so the trainer can replenish his kennel strength with younger and unexposed stock. In these circumstances it may be that the ageing greyhound is cast aside and even becomes unwanted.

The majority of greyhounds love to run, and if a greyhound is well maintained and has its injuries managed correctly, there is no reason why many can't run into their sixth or seventh year. While some trainers ridicule this notion, others see it as a training achievement to be able to sustain a dog's running ability for such a long time.

Managing the Veteran Racer at Home

The ageing greyhound will need to be trained in a slightly different manner to the youngster. Its ability to recover from a race will be a major factor, and when a dog starts heading for its fourth birthday it is time to abide by the 'once a week' rule. Running any dog twice a week on a regular basis is asking for trouble, but for the veteran it will probably spell disaster. You will notice that many older dogs are often tired or stiff the following day or two after a race, so it is important to let them recover in their own time. Running an older dog twice a week will only lead to stagnation, burnout or injury, so try and keep its runs to a *minimum* of seven days apart.

Another priority is making sure that the older dog is fed on a good diet and is given a supplement of vitamins and minerals. This may not make it run faster, but it will certainly help it recover from its races and will also help prevent injury.

It will be twice as important to check the dog thoroughly for any sign of injury. Old injuries can often become sore, so regular use of a magnetic field therapy unit can be vital to keeping the dog sound. I would have no qualms in putting a mature racer in the magnetic field therapy box on a daily basis even if it has no obvious or fresh injuries.

The ageing greyhound will also greatly benefit from regular massage. With daily massage its muscles can be kept toned, and this will also help with any stiffness and will help flush out any waste products from the muscles. Any dog that incurred an injury while in my care would have that injury treated on a daily basis. For example if it had a wrist injury, then that injury would be massaged and manipulated twice a day, every day, regardless of whether the dog was feeling any discomfort or not. If injuries are well managed, the prognosis for their improvement is much better.

The Veteran Racer on the Track

As much as I feel there is a place in greyhound racing for the older dog, I also think the tracks themselves could do more to help the ageing greyhound. While some tracks run races for puppies, very rarely do you see graded races aimed exclusively at the veteran. Furthermore, racing managers could also take into consideration the age of older dogs when grading a card, keeping them in the right boxes and not trying to overrun them. This could be a big help in keeping the ageing greyhound fit and injury free.

THE RETIRED GREYHOUND

There has always been a lot of finger pointing about whose responsibility it is to take care of the large number of retired greyhounds each year. While each owner has a responsibility to take care of, or find a home for, a dog on retirement, and although over the last few years a great deal more is being done by the sport in general to try and find homes for unwanted animals, I believe that the sport itself should make a greater contribution to the problem of retired greyhounds.

The root of the problem is that twenty years ago most tracks up and down the country were only allowed to race eight or ten race cards twice a week. However, racing has now increased four- or five-fold with the introduction of Bookmakers Afternoon Greyhound Service (BAGS) and Bookmakers Evening Greyhound Service (BEGS) meetings, which now take place seven days a week. This increase in meetings has also seen a big increase in races and dogs, with as many races as possible being squeezed in every day. While this is very profitable for the large bookmakers, the increase in the number of dogs they need to fill the race card means there are a lot more dogs that are raced out each year, which need to be rehomed.

The Greyhound as a Pet

On its retirement the greyhound can make a marvellous pet for both the younger and the more elderly owner, and any new owner of a retired greyhound can look forward to a lot of enjoyment. I myself have had retired greyhounds in the house and they can be as affectionate and loving and as much fun as any breed of dog.

When you first take your retired greyhound home it will probably take it a little while to adjust to its new way of life, and it may get quite stressed and pant heavily and whine. However, after a few days it should start to settle down. The racing greyhound has usually known nothing else but living in a kennel, so moving into a house can be quite a stressful change.

It is a good idea to set some ground rules right from the start. For instance, the dog should be given his own bedding area, and should not be allowed to sit on the furniture; if you do allow this kind of practice you will probably find that you end up sitting on the floor while the dog takes up the whole couch.

As the greyhound has never lived in a house before he is almost certainly going to need house training. Trying to teach a four-year-old dog a new habit is not always easy, so I recommend frequent trips to the garden and lots of praise and maybe a treat whenever he manages to empty out in the proper place. As time goes on the visits outside can be spaced wider apart, until the dog gets into a good routine.

When taking the greyhound for a walk always make sure you have the lead on correctly, and that the dog is muzzled for the first couple of weeks to prevent any nasty accidents with small dogs or cats. Generally when the greyhound has got out of the kennel environment it settles down remarkably well. Nevertheless, the new owner should always be aware that the greyhound has been purpose bred over the centuries to chase and kill.

The new owner will probably be surprised at how much his new friend likes to sleep. You might expect a greyhound to be very lively and full of energy: however, most will happily sleep all day and night if you let them, and when exercising there is no need to walk the legs off them – they will probably be quite happy with two or three light strolls a day. What I would suggest is that if you want to let your new dog off for a run, do so in an enclosed area, because if it bolts off after anything small and furry you may well have a job to catch it again.

Most greyhounds love children, and these feelings are usually mutual. However, no child should ever be allowed to tease or torment the

The retired greyhound is an affectionate and loving animal that can bring great pleasure to many a household. This loving breed is often seen as a dog that needs plenty of exercise, but contrary to belief the greyhound needs limited exercise in retirement.

A naughty greyhound takes a dip in the cold water.

Greyhounds, and especially old ones, love to sleep.

new addition to the family, nor is it a good idea to let a small child walk a greyhound or hold its lead, because if it sets off quickly the child is liable to be pulled right over.

Care and Maintenance

As a new owner you will want to look after your dog as well as you can. As regards diet, choose a good complete meal that is not too high in protein (about 15 per cent). The greyhound should be fed so he stays a few kilograms above his racing weight, but should not be allowed to get too fat. Never feed a greyhound on tinned dog food alone; the occasional tin of meat could be added for a bit of flavour, but no greyhound should be fed on tinned meat alone as this can affect its digestive system and weight.

During retirement it is important to keep an eye on the greyhound's teeth. Any bad ones should be removed by your veterinary surgeon, and as routine maintenance it is beneficial to brush the dog's teeth every day.

It is also still important that you worm the greyhound regularly, however I would suggest that once or twice a year should be sufficient once it has stopped racing.

If the greyhound is living indoors you shouldn't have too much of a problem with it moulting; the short-coated greyhound is unlikely to get too thick or prolific a coat in the winter months if it stays indoors. However, it does love the attention of being groomed, so brushing it every day will hopefully keep it happy. It is also a good idea to buy a flea comb and check for fleas on a regular basis; this is more important during the summer months when fleas are rife.

A Loving Family Pet

Greyhounds can sometimes be naughty when you take them home: emptying cupboards, pinching food, pulling curtains down, chewing furniture and eating the contents of your fridge may be some of the problems you have to deal with. However, with a bit of careful planning before you leave the house you should be able to get round most of them.

The age a greyhound lives to can vary a great deal; I have known some that have lived to seventeen years old, but equally I have known a lot of others pass on before they reach ten or eleven. The ageing greyhound often suffers from kidney problems, so keep an eye on his waterworks as he gets older. A large increase in water intake and trouble passing urine are two telltale signs of failing kidneys.

But all in all the greyhound can make an amazing and loving pet for the whole family to enjoy.

CHAPTER THIRTEEN

Buying and Selling a Greyhound

For the novice trainer or owner, deciding how and where to purchase a new greyhound can be quite a risky business. There are many different outlets for the purchase of a new greyhound: it could be an advertisement at the local track or in one of the racing papers, it could be from one of the greyhound sales that take place at certain tracks, or it could be through an agent or middleman.

For the ordinary man in the street £1,000 may seem a lot of money to spend on a dog, but in the greyhound world you would be lucky to get anything more than a decent grader or average dog for this amount. If you want to purchase a quality greyhound to compete in open events you are going to have to spend somewhere in the region of £2,000 to £3,000 minimum – and if you want a dog to contest the major competitions, then you could be talking telephone numbers because dogs regularly change hands for £10,000 or £20,000.

The majority of owners and trainers deal with the graded greyhounds that race up and down the country on a day-to-day basis. These lower graded dogs can often be purchased quite cheaply, and a moderate grader can often be bought for £500 and a low grader for £200. Whatever your budget, there is usually a greyhound somewhere to suit everyone.

If you are buying a new greyhound, the first thing you need to decide is what sort of dog you would like to buy, and how much you want to spend. You may want to buy a puppy or you may want a more experienced dog; you may want a sprinter or a distance dog. Many people just enjoy the fact of buying a young, cheap dog and hoping that it will stay sound and hopefully improve and win a few races along the way.

In general the most expensive greyhounds are young dogs, under two years of age, that have already showed some ability, and greyhounds that are competing in open class events. Up to the age of around three years a greyhound should keep most of its value as long as it is sustaining its race form. Once it gets past the age of three its value may start to decrease, and this is often when owners move the dog on and invest in a younger one. It is in these circumstances that a good animal can be purchased for around £1,000, though at this age you have to be more careful that the dog is sound, and that it hasn't been abused and over-raced.

AGENTS

If you have been involved in dog racing for a while then you will probably get to know a few of the agents or sellers. Many of these dealers import a few greyhounds from Ireland and then sell them on, and while some work locally, there are others who work on a more national scale. These dealers often advertise in some of the national greyhound papers.

I personally used a local agent to purchase a lot of my graded dogs; the man was a colourful chap whom I had known from boyhood. He often referred to himself as 'Barry's bargain basement', and I purchased many good quality, cheap greyhounds from him over the years.

The novice trainer, or anyone who is new to the game, must understand that you can't expect to buy a dog for £300 and then win a top race with it. You must also realize that dogs go lame and fight; however, if you deal a lot with the same agent you may well find that they will exchange a dog that fights.

I was also lucky that one of my owners was in contact with a very good agent in the Manchester area. This guy would periodically get in touch and say that he had a very fast dog for sale at a reasonable price; he was an extremely good judge and was not often wrong, so if he said the dog was useful then it usually was. However, finding a dealer or agent who will not rip you off is not easy, and if you are a novice trainer you should ask about at your local track to try and establish who has a good reputation.

ADVERTISEMENTS

Many handlers purchase their dogs through advertisements in the racing papers; often the dog's age is given and a list of some of its best runs. I personally don't like buying a dog in this fashion unless I already know it or its seller, and have often advised owners against spending big money on greyhounds advertised in the paper; however, they rarely listen and often do as they please. Over the years I have turned away dogs bought in this manner because so often the owner can't understand why the dog is not performing up to expectations, and quite happily blames its lack of form on the trainer.

I am not trying to suggest that every dog bought through an advert is going to be a bad buy; there are many genuine people out there who may just want to move a dog on. However, it must be appreciated that some dogs are run beyond their natural capability to put up a fast race time so they can be sold well above their price.

When the dog is purchased it may well never produce the sort of runs that you expect it to.

If you are a novice it is easy to get sucked in, and all I would advise is that you are very careful when parting with your hard-earned cash.

GREYHOUND SALES

There are greyhound sales that take place around England and Ireland most of the year round. The greyhound's books are made available for punters so they can look at what it has done previously, and then the dogs are trialled and auctioned off. Buying a greyhound from a sale can be as much luck as good judgement; however, here are a few pointers:

- If you like the look of a dog, watch it very closely for signs of fighting; dogs at sales often have a reputation for having bad traits. When the hare is whisked away, watch for any messing after the trial is over.
- Watch the dog walk off the track and look for any sign of lameness.
- When the greyhound you want to buy is on the stand, try and observe it as best you can.
- Make your mind up what you think a dog is worth, and stick to it; if it goes over what you think, leave it alone.
- Don't buy a greyhound for the sake of buying one; if there is nothing that takes your fancy, save your money for another day.

POINTERS WHEN BUYING A DOG

If an owner wants me to purchase an expensive dog, I like to try and abide by the following guidelines – if my head is on the chopping block then I like to make sure that everything is 'spot on'. If the seller had a problem with any of my requests I would usually be sceptical about purchasing the greyhound.

- If possible you want to see the dog run in person; an unofficial trial can often be arranged so that you can maybe run it against one of your own animals as a guide to how good it is. If the dog is already graded on a track you can travel to the course and watch it run.
- After you have seen the dog run, it is wise to examine it for any signs of injury. While mild soreness or small injuries will be not much of a problem, any old or serious scarring may be.

What you need to be looking for are any old injuries in problem areas: the wrist, the gracalis, the TFL and the Achilles tendon; injuries to these areas can end a greyhound's career, so any damage should give you food for thought. If you are a novice and are spending a large sum of money on a dog, then you may be advised to have someone with a little more experience to check the dog for you.

- It is important to check the greyhound's official race card or Irish book. Never buy a greyhound off one flash Irish time, because it may be that the dog did a phenomenal run on a very fast track and may never put in a time like it again.
- Educate yourself on the tracks, and what constitutes as being a good run at each one. Different tracks often run the same distance races; for example in Ireland they run a lot of 525yd races. However, at each track a fast time can vary a great deal, so it is advisable to learn something about race times at each track.
- Check the dog's race card for any long lay-off periods; if there is a gap of four or five months, then you need to be asking why the dog was laid up. In Ireland some handlers like to put their good dogs away for the winter.
- In general, young greyhounds have a lot of improvement in them; greyhounds under twenty months of age often have plenty of scope. However, be cautious if a puppy has been heavily raced, or has been run frequently at an independent track before it comes of age, because in this case there may be little improvement and the dog may burn out quickly.
- When buying a young dog I like to buy one of around eighteen months old that has only two or three runs on its card. I also prefer it to look a little out of condition and rough around the edges, because if a pup looks in pristine condition then you may struggle to bring it on, or to improve it as much as you would like.
- Never buy a greyhound on looks. I have seen some small, skinny and weedy dogs that can run like the wind, and I have also seen some beautiful, made up greyhounds that were completely useless. Never judge a book by its cover.
- Don't be put off buying older greyhounds; you can often pick up some very useful animals that have passed their third birthday. Many of the top trainers like to replenish their stock as they feel some of their older dogs are fully exposed. When buying an older dog you may well find that they have an injury or two to cope with, and this is when your knowledge of injuries and how to nurse them can be of great benefit.
- As with anything in life, there is always an element of luck in purchasing a greyhound.

BUYING A PUPPY

Many handlers like to buy a puppy or sapling at a very early age. Purchasing a puppy at ten weeks old, and then rearing it, can be a lot less expensive than trying to rear a litter from one of your own bitches. Handlers who have never seen a greyhound puppy are often surprised at how unlike a greyhound it looks – it is often fat and round and looks anything but a miniature greyhound.

When purchasing a puppy from a litter it is often the largest pups that are considered to be the best. However, I would suggest that it is impossible to pick the best out of a litter at an early age as the pups will develop at a different rate. You often hear tales of someone who has bought the last pup in a litter for next to nothing, usually the one that nobody wants because it is small and weak – yet it is often this pup that turns out to be a flying machine and the best of the litter.

Some handlers won't buy certain types of pup – one with blue eyes, or a dark muzzle, or a curly tail. Well, over the years there have been many top class dogs with these traits, so I would pay little attention to the myths that often surround certain types of dog.

For a novice owner – or indeed any owner – I would be very sceptical about paying a large amount of money for a pup. By this I mean that buying a dog at four or five months old for thousands of pounds is a very risky business. While some pups have the credentials to be top class greyhounds, you must take into consideration some important facts:

- Out of a litter of ten you are likely to get two or three of the pups that either don't chase or will play and fight and never make the track.
- Three or four of the pups are likely to be slow or mediocre and will never make much more than a grader.
- If you are very lucky you may get one or two good class greyhounds out of the one litter.

Over the years there have been some highly reputable breeders who do turn out a high percentage of good class greyhounds because they have quality breeding bitches bred from their own bloodlines. But these breeders are few and far between, and very rarely sell any potential brood bitches.

I have seen many novice owners purchase a pup for a large amount of money who tell me how good their dog is going to be and that it will be open class. They are often taken aback if you tell them not to be too hopeful about the dog being as good as they envisage. If you are new to the game it is easy to be taken in by a salesman with a plausible sales patter.

If you intend to spend a lot of money on a young pup, my advice is to check out the dam line yourself. This can be done easily on the internet. Check how good the mother and her siblings were; even if the mother was not particularly fast she may well belong to a very classy litter. Check out the dam's parents, and how many quality siblings they had: if there are quality dogs on the dam's side then the pup may well have a lot of potential. But it is important not to just jump in and buy a pup for a lot of money and expect the price tag to do the talking.

SELLING A DOG

It is quite amazing that whenever you want to buy a dog, those for sale always seem to be over-priced, but if you want to sell one, no one wants to give you what you think it is worth. Unfortunately that's just a part of the sport.

If you have a fast dog, the best place to sell is usually in the national paper. However, if you have a very good dog, when people know that it is up for sale you are likely to receive offers. Indeed, if you have an exceptional dog, people will quite often make you an offer even if you don't want to sell.

So how much is a dog worth? Although some people like to boast about a dog being worth X pounds, a dog is actually only worth as much as someone is willing to pay for it. So be realistic about how much you want to sell your dog for; if it is an older dog then the price will be a lot less than what you maybe paid for it, even if it is still running well.

Glossary

anti-oxidants Prevent fats and oils from becoming rancid when they are exposed to air.

bitch A female dog.

brindle Striped like a tiger.

catch its tongue Let the dog get its breath back and stop panting excessively.

collar [a dog] up Putting a lead and collar on to a dog's neck.

coloured dog A dog that is of more than one substantial colour; being marked like a dairy cow.

condition/conditioning To bring a dog to peak physical fitness.

cycle A period of time or a recurring period of time.

dew claw The small number one toe situated on the inner foreleg. On rare occasions a dog has a dew claw or claws on the hind feet.

DMG A metabolic enhancer used to improve the immune system, the cardiovascular system and muscle performance.

dog A male dog.

electrolytes Used to replace lost body salts after a hard race or after any strong physical activity.

fibrous/fibre up When the tissue becomes thicker and firmer around an injury. This is often seen in injuries as they heal, and can also be known as scar tissue.

form A description of the dog's most recent races.

gait The dog's action whilst walking or running.

good healthy back/good back A good covering of muscle across the back (not fat), with the back and hip bones just showing.

groin The muscle that runs on the inside of the inner leg; the majority of the muscle is concealed, but the top can be seen and felt as a small triangular muscle situated at the top inner thigh.

hare trip Where the hare finishes at the end of the race.

hose off, to Using a hose pipe to apply cold water to an injury.

ice pack A frozen substance such as a bag of frozen peas. It is used to reduce inflammation and swelling around a fresh injury such as a bruise.

illegal substances May cause a positive sample if the dog is drug tested.

insertion of the muscle/tendon Where the muscle or the tissue attaches to the bone.

joint The coming together of two or more bones.

kaolin Substance used for treating several problems, including drawing poison from a wound, softening thick tissue around a joint, and applying heat to an injury such as a sprained wrist.

let [a dog] down/come down Allowing a dog to train off by reducing its workload and diet.

lie of the coat The direction in which the hair or coat runs.

MFT Magnetic field therapy.

muscle belly The thick part or centre of the muscle.

muscle sheath The thin layer of tissue that encases a muscle.

NGRC National Greyhound Racing Club.

pick up injuries detect injuries that your greyhound has sustained.

plain dog A dog that is one colour such as black or brindle.

post race The time after a race.

pre-race The time prior to a race.

quick The thin layer of blood that is encased in the nail.

restricted movement Describes the shortfall in movement of a joint.

run off To lose weight.

run out of its skin To run extremely well, or run as well as the dog ever has in a race or trial.

scapula Shoulder blade.

scarred tissue The result of damage to a muscle or tendon. The tissue will feel old and firm, and can also be described as fibrous tissue.

schooling track A track that is used for the purpose of schooling young greyhounds; may also be used to give unofficial trials to gain information on the fitness and performance of one's greyhound.

slip, to To hold on to a dog and physically let it go by hand.

slip the collar A dog that pulls his head through the collar.

slips Two adjoining leather leads that the greyhounds starts from in a coursing event.

spirit blister Solution that is generally a split of iodine and surgical spirit, used to create a reaction on application. The blister usually swells and warms the affected area, causing a constant draw of bloodflow to the area.

standing square Making the dog stand straight and bearing equal weight on all four limbs.

straddle To stand over the dog around its mid-section.

stud dog A male dog used for the purpose of impregnating bitches.

surgical spirits Alcohol-based substance used for several ailments in the greyhound. Most commonly it can be massaged into the greyhound to improve circulation and blood-flow into the muscles.

TCP Brand name of an antiseptic solution that has many benefits.

TFL Tensor fascia lata muscle.

tendon A strong piece of tissue that usually is associated with attaching muscle to bone.

tendonous attachment Location where a tendon attaches to the bone.

trial Pre-race run involving any number of dogs to test the dog's ability. Most tracks insist that a greyhound has a minimum of three trials before it can be entered in a graded race. Trials are also used to bring dogs back to fitness after an injury or lay-off.

vitamins Essential for the normal growth and development of a greyhound, or indeed any animal. Dietary supplements are often used to ensure that adequate amounts of nutrients are obtained on a daily basis, if the optimal amounts cannot be obtained through the dog's diet.

Index